Praise for *Beyond The*

"Great leadership entails being an influencer of people. Jim has captured this beautifully in his book *Beyond Theory and Degrees: The Alley Smarts of Educational Leadership* with his authentic storytelling of his leadership experiences. Jim's encouraging voice reminds us that we all can learn and should learn from one another in our respective leadership roles. He candidly shares the need for all leaders to develop confidence, self-discipline, and resilience as the tools for successful leadership. This book is a practical reflection of various entry points into leadership as an aspiring or practicing leader. Most importantly, Jim reminds us of the importance of relationships not only to one another but also to a place of shared responsibilities and benefits to serve all children and families and serve them well through our excellent leadership."

—Deb Kerr, 2019–2020 president, American Association of School Administrators; superintendent, Brown Deer School District, Wisconsin

"This book is a must-read for aspiring school administrators. It is also a valuable 'refresher' for veteran administrators who want to be reminded of the essential principles of their profession so that they can lead and mentor their administrative teams. Dr. Fitzpatrick has captured the essence of what it takes to be a successful school leader. Read it and you will have a solid foundation for your career in the noble profession of school administration."

—Miles Turner, retired executive director, Wisconsin Association of School District Administrators

"*Beyond Theory and Degrees: The Alley Smarts of School Leadership* distills what is great about Dr. Fitzpatrick's teaching, including his legendary sense of humor, and puts it in an accessible package. Now everyone can benefit from his mentorship and practical wisdom!"

—Ryan McCarty, PhD, assistant professor, National Louis University

Beyond Theory and Degrees

The Alley Smarts of Educational Leadership

James E. Fitzpatrick

Foreword by Governor Jim Doyle

ROWMAN & LITTLEFIELD
Lanham • Boulder • New York • London

Published by Rowman & Littlefield
An imprint of The Rowman & Littlefield Publishing Group, Inc.
4501 Forbes Boulevard, Suite 200, Lanham, Maryland 20706
https://rowman.com

6 Tinworth Street, London SE11 5AL, United Kingdom

British Library Cataloguing in Publication Information Available

Library of Congress Cataloging-in-Publication Data
Names: Fitzpatrick, James E., author.
Title: Beyond theory and degrees : the alley smarts of educational leadership / James E.
    Fitzpatrick.
Description: Lanham, Maryland : Rowman & Littlefield, 2020. | Includes bibliographical
    references.
Identifiers: LCCN 2020001218 (print) | LCCN 2020001219 (ebook) | ISBN
    9781475851076 (cloth) | ISBN 9781475851083 (paperback) | ISBN 9781475851090
    (epub)
Subjects: LCSH: Educational leadership—United States. | School management and organ-
    ization—United States. | School districts—United States—Administration
Classification: LCC LB2805 .F54 2020 (print) | LCC LB2805 (ebook) | DDC 371.2—
    dc23
LC record available at https://lccn.loc.gov/2020001218
LC ebook record available at https://lccn.loc.gov/2020001219

Contents

Contents

Foreword

I love Wisconsin public schools. During my two terms as governor, education was my top priority. I have had the great privilege of working with many great teachers and administrators. In communities big and small, I have seen the importance of strong, thoughtful, and collaborative leaders.

Jim "Fitz" Fitzpatrick was one of those great leaders. He served as a superintendent and principal in Wisconsin from 1986 to 2013. I got to know Fitz after my election as governor in 2002. Over the next eight years, we worked together to see that schools were adequately and equitably funded and fought against efforts to slash school budgets. My wife, Jessica, an educator herself, visited his district on several occasions.

Fitz has been, and continues to be, a passionate and effective advocate for education in the cities in which he worked, throughout the state of Wisconsin and across the country. As the outstanding superintendent in Fort Atkinson, and a beloved high school principal in Beloit, he provided caring leadership, tirelessly driven to provide opportunities, service, and access to all students. Widely respected by his peer principals and superintendents, he often served as a mentor to many of them. Communities where he served remain deeply in his debt and remember him fondly.

Fitz has now written a book from the lens of a practitioner in which he shares his experiences in building a strong learning culture. His insights extend beyond what is taught in educational leadership programs. He shares a common sense approach to building relationships and garnering educator, parent, and community support for schools. His book is a blueprint for success for aspiring administrators and practicing leaders who may be motivated to take the next step in their careers. As you turn the pages, you gain an appreciation for his down to earth approach, humor, and understanding of the leadership process.

Now an educational leadership professor at National Louis University in Chicago, Fitz continues his leadership work. In teaching and mentoring aspiring school leaders and doctoral candidates in both the classroom and internships, Fitz not only shares leadership theory but also the "alley smarts" he picked up along his journey. From his preface to the last chapter on life balance, you will find his leadership nuggets interesting and helpful.

This book is a must-read that will appeal to a wide audience. In addition to aspiring school leaders, Fitz's book would provide an insightful book study for administrative teams, Board of Education members, and anyone with an interest in school leadership and governance.

Jim Doyle
Governor of Wisconsin, 2003–2011

Jim Doyle. Photo courtesy of Foley Law Offices, Madison, Wisconsin.

Preface

What I Can Offer You in Your Quest to Be an Educational Leader

Having read many books that were helpful to me in shaping my thoughts and views on life, education, and leadership, I often wondered if I could pay it forward, do the same, and write a book that could be helpful to others. My fear in contemplating such an endeavor was to ask myself, "Do I really have something to offer that would be worth someone reading?"

Well, after forty-four years in private and public education, I have climbed the ranks of teacher, coach, principal, superintendent, and now university professor. I have served in rural, suburban, and urban communities. So I am hoping I may have something to offer beyond the academic underpinning of theory and best practices taught to us in university and college leadership programs.

So I am taking the plunge in hoping I can help aspiring and current administrators. I cannot express adequately in words how blessed I have been to have great mentors. In a way this book is a tribute to all of the people who helped shape my life and my profession. I hope this book can serve as a helpful reference and provide some informal mentoring as I touch on several different topics and challenges we face as educational leaders.

This is not a scholarly work by any means. You will discover that soon enough as you turn the pages. However, it is an attempt to share some thoughts in a common sense manner on how a person can become an impactful leader if there is a passion to serve youth and build leaders around you.

In my journey I have learned that it isn't always the brightest, high IQ leaders who make the greatest difference; it is those leaders who are truly invested in the learning communities they serve! These leaders have fire in their belly that makes everyone around them understand they are *all in*!

I am often in awe of intellectually gifted authors and educational leaders who have a great command of the language and can present their message seemingly effortlessly. They can tell a story that hooks us right away. While my message in this book will lack this eloquence and acumen, I promise you it is genuine and from the heart. I present my thoughts for your consideration as you reflect upon your leadership philosophy and practice. As I tell my educational leadership students, "take what you like and leave the rest."

In closing, I grew up in the Chicago area, one of eight children. In our Irish Catholic family, you learned to never be late for dinner, get in and out of the only bathroom in five minutes, make your bed, and say your prayers at night. From these humble beginnings I share my observations in this book, not as a scholar but as a school man who learned a few things during my journey that I did not learn from books and lectures. If you have gotten this far, thanks for reading, and I hope there are some takeaways you gather from this book. If that happens, well, I am glad I could help you!

Introduction

This book is organized into three parts and in an ascending order. It is intended to give the reader a nontheoretical view of school governance from building leadership up through Board governance. The book is an attempt to inspire those who may be considering taking the next step in their educational careers. Teachers considering moving into administration and principals pondering a move to a superintendency or a central office role all might benefit from reading this book. Others who have a keen interest in the governance and operations of schools and districts can also come away with some new perspectives as seen through the lens of a career practitioner.

Part I is designed to hook readers into understanding they can be impactful school leaders. Too many people who have the potential to become great leaders fear they might not have what it takes to lead. This is sad because never before in our history have we had a greater need for exemplary school leaders!

In this early section of the book, the processes of leadership are discussed as the keys to leadership success. More than scholarly acumen, it is an understanding of how to build a culture of affirmation, collaboration, and trust that serves as the underpinning of the caring leadership we need in our learning communities today.

Part II gives insight into the ever evolving role of the principal. In building a culture of leaders, a principal can empower staff to accept and flourish in leadership roles. In this section of the book, current practice is challenged as it relates to teacher evaluation and the premise that principals who are good managers are not good leaders.

The most important evaluation a principal ever completes is at the point of hire! It isn't enough to hire great people; you must continuously help them grow. Too often after recruitment, interviewing, and selecting people, we fail to provide a proper induction in helping the new teacher assimilate into the school culture.

The key point discussed in part II is to raise the conscious level of readers on just how important the principal is in helping a school flourish. A principal who is accessible, visible, and a good listener supports the teachers and staff. A principal makes sure that noncertified staff are held accountable like teachers and are equally respected for the roles they play.

In part III the book moves into the superintendency and the Board of Education. This section begins with commentary on how a candidate should approach landing a superintendent job. Later, a metaphorical analogy of the superintendent being compared to an NFL head coach is discussed, along with the development of a strategic plan that is composed of an academic agenda, a fiscal agenda, and communication agenda.

The roles of chief academic officers and chief finance officers are analyzed as they relate to responsibilities and boundaries and how a superintendent builds a cohesive leadership team. Meetings, keeping a pulse on the district, and planning for Board meetings are discussed.

Moving on to the Board of Education (BOE) and the superintendent and their respective roles and relationships, there is a strong emphasis placed on the boundaries each plays in the shared governance roles. The Board of Education, duly elected by the citizens, determines the what! This is the adoption of policy and oversight of the district. In both policy and oversight a Board of Education should be focused on student achievement and continuous improvement. That is the what!

The superintendent and his or her educational team are responsible for the how! Once the Board determines the what (which includes approval of the Strategic Plan), the next step is for the superintendent and the educational team to figure out the how through the development of desired outcomes, annual goals, and action plans.

Shared governance succeeds when the BOE and the superintendent "stay in their yards." Board members do not engage in micromanaging, and superintendents do not decide policy.

The book closes with a very important chapter focusing on life balance. A case study is presented that provokes one to step back and analyze how one currently balances personal life and work and what could be at stake if in fact the job is all consuming. Suggestions are made on how balance can be achieved.

A final thought on how this book can be used. Each chapter approaches a specific leadership topic. In addition to this book being discussed as a whole, it can also be a valuable resource for breaking out parts and chapters for administrative team book studies or class engagement topics in educational leadership courses.

A goal of the author was to provide the readers with something new and interesting that might advance their thoughts, views, and understanding of educational leadership. Moreover, if it motivates an educator to take his or her career to the next level, that would be great! The future of our schools depends on caring and invested leaders stepping up to accept these roles. You can do it!

Part I

The Essentials of Leadership

Chapter One

Do I Have the Pedigree to Lead?

When contemplating whether one wants to make the transition from the faculty ranks to administration it is not unusual to have some feelings of self-doubt. Even as educators begin working toward an administrative license, they often wonder, "Can I do this?"

Yes, you can!

One of the ways to assure yourself is to think back and remember the mentors you had during your journey. What was it they saw in you that made you feel good about seeking their wisdom and embracing their advice? Have you ever asked yourself why they took the time to really invest in you?

Of course when we think of people who have influenced us we often start with our parents. As much as anyone our parents have had the greatest influence on us. The beliefs they instilled in us have a long-lasting impact. It's not until early adolescence that others aside from our parents begin to influence our views and attitudes. We often become adults before we truly appreciate the love and guidance our parents provided.

During adolescence we begin to contrast what our parents have taught us and what we are beginning to learn from sixth grade on. While we might have some streaks of rebellion, the influence of our parents has deep roots.

MENTORS

There are not many self-made people. Aside from our parents, when asked who had the greatest influence on them, people invariably respond that it was a teacher, coach, or educator! These were school people who inspired our best efforts and often demanded no less. And when we achieved and succeeded, we gained confidence! To influence someone so profoundly is deeply rewarding to a mentor. Leaders get to be mentors. They have the wonderful opportunity to build teams of difference makers.

A retired superintendent who came up through the teaching, coaching, and principal ranks reflected on his journey. He talked about how educators and coaches gave him opportunities to gain confidence through success. He remembers the self-discipline, resilience, and kindness they modeled and instilled in him. He recalled fondly his freshman world history and homeroom teacher in the Catholic high school he attended. This teacher was assigned the lowest track of students based on the ninth-grade admission exam.

"Mr. Pauls was like a stern Gabe Kaplan from the Welcome Back, Kotter *show that aired in the mid-seventies. Heck, we all knew we were in the lowest track. The funny thing that most of us learned later was that he was brought in to be the varsity basketball coach. He was a physical education major who taught physical education except for our ninth-grade world history section.*

"The sharper kids were taught by two very academically grounded history teachers who were not nearly as strict. The principal wisely thought he needed a tough guy to handle us. Pauls had the hell scared out of all of us, yet he connected with us in a way we knew he was our champion! You wanted to please him.

"Pauls relied on the text as his curriculum that had an accompanying work book. At the end of the semester there was a ninth-grade world history exam competition. Pauls pulled several of us aside and very bluntly stated 'I want you guys to study your asses off and do our homeroom and world history class proud.'

"I had the highest score of all 180 freshmen. Five of the ten highest scores were Pauls's guys! It was only later that I realized Pauls himself may have had something to prove to his department colleagues and the principal! It wasn't that we loved history. We wanted to please Pauls because he believed in us! He gave us self-worth. The smile on his face when he saw the top ten scores is something we all remember! We forgot about being the lowest track, we now had confidence that we could flourish as high school students."

A second example of a wonderful mentor the superintendent recalled was his high school cross-country coach his senior year. He shared the following.

"By the end of my junior year I was a better than average distance runner winning my share of races. There is that old saying, 'you don't know what you don't know.' That could not have been truer! Enter Coach Bob Hoppenstedt, my cross-country coach my senior year!

"Hoppy, as we referred to him, came in with a reputation of getting the most out of his cross-country and track teams. From day one he promised that in ten weeks (the length of a fall cross-country season) we were going to run the best races of our lives if we stuck with him. He put us through some

grueling workouts that resulted in several guys quitting. However, for me the victories came in dual meets, and I finished seventh in the conference meet (compared to thirty-fifth the year before)! He instilled self-discipline, grit, and again confidence that I could tackle difficult transitions and challenges!"

A third wonderful influence the retired superintendent recalled was Sister Thomas Francis.

"She was an academic, really sharp and engaging! She taught a course called Senior Social Studies that was really a combination of economics and sociology. Sister caught me after class one day and asked me why I was not contributing to discussions. I confessed to her that I was a bit intimidated and afraid of making a fool of myself. There were some really smart kids in this class. She said, 'Okay, but every once in a while if you have an opinion I want to see your hand up.'

"Well you know what Sister Thomas Francis was really good at? She paid attention to student accomplishments in extracurricular activities. So once the bell rang for her class to start, the first thing she would do is acknowledge students in the class for sports, drama, music, etc. She made a point of really building me up when I won a cross-country race or when I received all-conference honors. She had the gift of affirming people. This also got me to raise my hand and not worry about what others might think of my comments. Her kindness in affirming her students is something that influenced me greatly. In my career I wanted to pay this forward."

In summary, like the superintendent here, we all have mentors in our journey who have instilled confidence in our ability to accomplish great things. You have made successful transitions already in your life from high school to college to a career. You have gained confidence, self-discipline, and resilience. You have been the fortunate recipient of kindness and respect that you can now pay forward.

When you think about it, there are not many roles more important in our society than school and district leadership. In answer to the question, "Do you have the pedigree?" the answer is most definitely! You are ready for this honorable and prestigious calling. Now it is time for you to take your game to the next level. You can be a positive difference maker in the lives of youths, educators, families, and communities. Yes, that can be you!

SUMMARY QUESTIONS TO PONDER

- Think back to your childhood and adolescence. What accomplishment gave you the most satisfaction and confidence?
- What would your spouse, friends, and fellow employees say is your greatest quality in working with others?

- What do you think your greatest mentors saw in you that made them want to invest their time in you?
- What would hold you back in assuming a school leadership role?

Chapter Two

Everything Starts with Culture

Peter Drucker, often acclaimed as the founder of modern management per his many scholarly writings, is credited with the saying, "Culture eats strategy for breakfast every day." For sure having a cohesive working environment and a positive culture is crucial in businesses and learning communities. So how do you build culture as a new leader coming in?

GETTING STARTED IN BUILDING A
POSITIVE AND VIBRANT CULTURE

Whether you are coming in as a new principal or superintendent there are some key questions you want to pose to stakeholders as you begin your new job. These questions will give you an early assessment of the present culture. They will provide you with insight as you begin your principalship or superintendency.

These five questions should be sent to all certified and noncertified staff as you begin a new job. The questionnaire should be anonymous, but you will be surprised by how many will share their names. In addition to the questions listed here, there should be a section for respondents to check indicating their roles (specifically teachers, counselors, aides, etc.).

If you are the incoming superintendent, you would also add a section regarding the building or department in which an employee serves. This questionnaire could be sent by US mail with a return postage paid envelope, survey monkey, or any online questionnaire format.

THE FIVE KEY QUESTIONS

- Question 1: What are the strengths of the school (or district)?
- Question 2: What might be areas that need some attention or improvement?
- Question 3: If you had a problem, personal or professional, who might you confide in at your school (or in the district)?
- Question 4: Who are the parents, community members, or business leaders who have been strong supporters of our school (or district)?
- Question 5: In looking forward to working with you as your new principal (or superintendent), is there anything else you would like to share with me at this time?

Question 1 will immediately inform you of the strengths, rituals, and traditions that are a sense of pride in a learning community. This is very important for a new administrator to learn and understand quickly. A mistake many leaders make is to come in with their own agenda while ignoring the cultural richness that may already exist and should be embraced.

Question 2 will yield a tremendous amount of information regarding some things that are not going well. Note how the question is phrased. The word *weaknesses* is not used for fear of offending; however, weaknesses and feelings of discontent are exactly what you will discover, especially when you see recurring comments on a number of questionnaires.

Question 3 will immediately tell you who the influential leaders are on staff and where the power resides. As a principal or superintendent you learn that it is difficult to succeed if you are unable or reluctant to delegate. In building a distributive leadership approach, which builds culture, this question informs you of who on the current staff has the confidence and trust of others. These are the people who can help you gain relational trust as you begin. Invariably you will see recurring names pop up.

One might assume that if a teacher had a professional problem he or she might confide in either the principal or union representative in his or her building. While this is often the case, you will discover that others on the staff are sought out. These are the informal leaders. There is a difference between *power* and *authority*. Title may give you authority but not necessarily influence and power. The responses to this question will give a new leader insight into who the informal leaders with influence are.

Question 4 will give you a knowledge base of parents, community members, and business people who understand the importance of the school or the school system in the community. On making a list of names that teachers and staff recorded as supportive, your next step would be to reach out to these parents and community leaders. Ask them to respond to questions 1, 2, 4, and 5.

Parents and community members may list some new names that faculty and staff did not identify. When you contrast the internal and external responses, you will find some common ground, some differences, and a few surprises per how employees and external stakeholders view the school or district. You will also learn how relationally connected the schools and the community are. This is a good thing to know early on!

Question 5 will render you a plethora of opinions and thoughts not covered in the previous four questions. You will be amazed at what employees and community members will share with you!

This survey is a way to really expedite your knowledge base in the first six to eight weeks you are on the job.

A next step would be to invite people in. As a principal, with the help of your administrative assistant, invite seven or eight people in at a time. This will allow you to introduce yourself more personally and have attendees share with you their backgrounds. More than likely the attendees will carry the conversation, and herein lies the importance of you being a *good listener*.

At these meetings, you also want to convey to attendees how excited you are to begin working with them. Notice the emphasis on working *with* them. It sets a collaborative tone. Early on you want to build rapport and establish relationships. The desired outcome of these meetings is that you want attendees to walk away feeling that their new leader was genuinely interested in what was shared.

This shortcut to gaining a lot of information is a great way to begin. While many administrative contracts begin on July 1 or August 1, the steps mentioned can help a new principal get off to a running start.

HOW TO SUSTAIN A POSITIVE CULTURE

Leaders begin building culture by first openly modeling their own sense of humility. Some leaders are really fearful of this, as if it were a weakness. Two of the most powerful words in the English language are "I'm sorry." Openly admitting to a mistake is really difficult for some leaders. I love the following quote from John Wooden, the Hall of Fame basketball coach of UCLA who led his teams to ten NCAA championships: "Talent is God given. Be humble. Fame is man-given. Be grateful. Conceit is self-given. Be careful."

To be clear, leaders have to make good decisions, be reflective, and not repeat mistakes. However, as a leader, no matter how talented you are, you will make mistakes. Acknowledge them and when necessary express your contriteness and move on. Author David Wolfe shared the following: "a mistake that makes you humble is better than an achievement that makes you arrogant." People are far more willing to follow a humble leader than they are a bright but arrogant leader who is afraid to admit mistakes.

INTEGRITY: ONCE YOU LOSE IT, YOU MAY NEVER GET IT BACK

When you lead a learning community, the most important trait followers want from their leaders is honesty. Faculty and staff want you to be candid with them, even when the news is bad or perhaps embarrassing for the leader and the learning community. Being transparent and sharing openly with stakeholders lends credibility. Educators and staff do not expect a leader to be perfect, but they do expect honesty.

Some leaders withhold information or only share it with certain people perceived as favorites. This creates great angst and resentment. Pretty soon unhealthy alliances and factions can form with a very negative impact on the culture. The truth always comes out in the end. It is far better for leaders to always be honest and transparent. Nothing defines us more than our integrity.

CELEBRATIONS CAN BUILD CONNECTEDNESS

Celebrations and partaking in joyful and fun activities interspersed throughout the school year can really add life and vitality to the culture. A school year is like a marathon. Some fun activities include short faculty skits or activities throughout the year when spirits are lifted and people are recognized for their accomplishments.

One of the things a new principal should take advantage of is the tremendous amount of talent your faculty and staff may possess. Not just your music and arts people who certainly can help you, but others who once in a while enjoy being corny and performing. There are a lot of Walter Mittys out there!

You want to build a culture where people want to come to your faculty celebrations and recognitions. As a leader, while you may delegate to others in helping you pull off a celebration, it is important for the leader to share gratitude and affirmation for the good work in opening and closing remarks.

Sometimes you do not need a real organized program to bring staff together. Food is always a good incentive. February and March are the steep hills of the marathon school year. This is a good time to have a celebration or social activity. It is also a good time for the leaders to remind their staff how grateful they are for all of the collective efforts being put forth in the learning community.

In short, never miss an opportunity to affirm. You always want to keep a pulse on the energy and stress levels of your staff. Celebrations and messages from the leader affirming the troops goes a long way to everyone feeling they are valued and appreciated.

HUMOR

Humor is often undervalued in a learning community. As mentioned, there are some very talented and funny people on your staff. While leadership is a serious business, taking time to laugh and have some fun is really important in building culture.

As an example, a superintendent was walking the halls of an elementary building where the district office was located at one end. He came across a group of third-grade boys, including his little neighbor Nick, who greeted him by calling him doctor. As he turned the corner he heard one little fellow ask, "Is he really a doctor?" Nick clarified by saying, "Yeah, he is a doctor but a different kind. If you broke your arm he could not do a thing for you." The superintendent often shared this little encounter in speeches and presentations, always getting a good laugh.

Some wise advice on your way up the ladder of your career would be to never take yourself too seriously. Again this is a reminder to stay humble. Sharing your sense of humor or showing your fun side puts the people you lead at ease. There are times when humor is exactly what is needed. School work is an intense business, and sometimes we need to stop and smell the roses.

Storytelling is a nice skill for a leader to have, especially when you can share a funny experience, often poking fun at yourself. For example, on one occasion an urban high school principal, in his haste to get an email out, found out the hard way that it helps to have a second set of eyes review a communication. In wanting to promote spirit among the staff, he sent out the following email blast: *"Faculty please remember to wear your SPIRIT SHIT on Friday."* He meant spirit shirt. His staff kiddingly never let him off the hook on that one!

GENUINENESS AND COMPASSION

It is often stated that people do not quit jobs, they quit bosses. Along with honesty, faculty and staff value a leader who is genuine and comfortable in his or her own skin. It does not take long for people (and especially school people) to detect phoniness. Leaders pretending to be someone other than their true selves are invariably exposed for who they really are. Teachers and staff also observe the degree to which a leader is committed to them. They quickly sniff out leaders who are just trying to build their résumé for their next career ladder jump.

School leaders must be invested in their people. Conveying a caring attitude toward staff is so important. Furthermore, it has to be genuine and sincere. This translates to taking the time to listen and getting to really know your people. Many teachers and administrators have left jobs to work in other districts for less money. The need to feel cared for and valued is something we all covet.

Teachers and staff you are working with have the same life experiences as anyone else. However, their sense of duty and commitment to the children and youth in their classrooms and schools rarely waivers. At times they put themselves and families second.

As a leader you need to know what might be going on for a faculty or staff member outside of school. Not in an overreaching or nosey manner but by keeping your ear to the ground. Maybe its aging parents with medical issues or children of their own who are struggling. Or maybe a death or divorce or some other life-changing event. In a learning community where there is trust, leaders learn from staff members themselves or their colleagues when someone is going through tough times.

VISIBILITY: GETTING OUT AND AROUND

Visibility and getting out of the office is one of the most important things a leader can do in sustaining a positive culture. You want students, staff, and parents to feel they see you often and that you care about them. This is hard to do if you are chained to your office desk. Emails, phone messages, and tasks can pile up, but you have to get out of your office.

One principal liked to "scoop the loop" as he called it and stop by and peak into every classroom and say hello or make eye contact with every teacher before school. This often resulted in some short impromptu conversations that kept him abreast of things in the building. If the exchange was going to take more than a minute, he would arrange a time when the teacher could meet with him at length, thus sending the message *I want to hear you out without distractions.*

As he cruised the halls saying hello to students, aides, custodians, and people passing, it gave them a chance to stop him if they had a concern or a question. Students would often ask if he was coming to the game, play, or concert that night. Scooping the loop, while seemingly a very simple action, gave him a *connection* with all in the building. He recalled, "Even in those short exchanges, some important information emerged!"

For a superintendent in charge of multiple buildings, it would be much harder to see all staff on a daily basis. However, it is important to get into buildings as frequently as possible so people will connect with you. One of the saddest commentaries teachers sometimes share is that they *do not know their superintendent.*

A good time for a superintendent to visit schools is right before class begins and at lunch times when you can cruise the halls and cafeterias. As important as it is for teachers and staff to know who you are, it is also important that students get to know and recognize you as well. One of the things you will truly miss if you transition to central office is being with the kids! So getting to musicals, games, and art shows are all things a superintendent should have on the calendar.

One superintendent after holiday concerts would stand by the door after the performance and thank parents and grandparents for coming. After retiring, this superintendent recalled a grandparent coming up to him and saying, "We miss seeing you at the concerts." Little things like this result in building a lot of goodwill between home and school. Another good event to have on the calendar is parent-teacher conferences. These are sometimes held arena style in a gymnasium or large space. You can meet and greet many parents and teachers at such an event or in cruising the halls if conferences are held in classrooms.

The kids, like the parents, really notice when the superintendent attends their activities. You want every kid to think his or her activity is very important to you. As a principal and a superintendent, you should try to attend as many activities as you possibly can. Of course you cannot make it to everything, but your attendance or lack of does not go unnoticed by the kids and their parents, coaches, club directors, music directors, and custodians. It's true that if the students feel favorably about an educator, then it is likely the parents will as well.

You want to leave the impression that Future Farmers of America is every bit as important as football, music, and forensics. In fact, getting to a cross-country meet or a forensics meet where there was often low spectatorship really reinforces for students, parents, and coaches that the principal or superintendent really cares about their interests.

While at the high school level there are many activities one could choose to attend as a superintendent, there are plentiful opportunities at the elementary and middle school buildings as well. Parents with kids at different levels often see you in multiple grade level settings and they will spread the word about your presence.

In addition to affirming the students in their activities, equally important is just getting to meet and know many parents and community members. In building a school culture you also want to be aware of contributing to the community culture. Being a member of a service club, a local church, and serving on the public library board and the local hospital board are examples of types of community involvement that provide a valuable connection between the schools and the community.

These connections can prove invaluable, especially when trying to pass referendums. One superintendent encouraged all of his administrators to live in the community. He encouraged them to be involved in at least one community organization, along with patronizing the local businesses. Purchasing cars, gas, and groceries locally gets noticed! As does coaching Little League, Scout leadership, and worshiping in a local church. School administrators are some of the highest paid people in towns of thirty thousand or less. This is not only a way to establish relationships and make connections but also a way to give back in supporting the community.

THE LITTLE GENUINE THINGS MEAN A LOT

In sustaining a culture, I believe the best leaders grasp that people are more important than process. In a given year many things can happen within a learning community, and if the culture is not strong, things can deteriorate. Here are some things that can really make a difference in building and maintaining relationships.

- Sending a congratulatory note when a teacher or staff member experiences the birth of a child.
- Sending a note of best wishes for an upcoming marriage.
- Publicly recognizing honors and accomplishments of people on your staff. In addition, sending a nice personal note. People will save them as they mean a lot!
- Taking time to celebrate school (or district) accomplishments and milestones. Sometimes it seems sad if we only celebrate people when they retire. There may have been intervals during their careers when acknowledgment and affirmation might have been just what they needed.
- Attending visitations or funerals when someone in the learning community loses a loved one. If this is impossible because of distance, a handwritten note of condolence with a memorial check enclosed conveying sympathy is a kind and important gesture.
- You will have staff members who are working through a divorce or a breakup. Knowing the boss cares goes a long way. Just a simple note stating "thinking of you" is a thoughtful gesture that validates your concern and care!
- Interpreting the master bargaining agreement: be as flexible and reasonable as possible. That will serve you well. Most teachers and staff will remember this and go the extra mile for you.

GIVE EVERYONE A CHANCE TO LEAD AND SHINE

A basketball coach once conveyed a story regarding his frustration with his basketball team and their failure to run the half-court offense. He finally stood up, called a time-out, and angrily sat his players down. He then told them that on the next possession he wanted them to run the offense. He did not want to see a shot go up until every player "got a touch."

In using this same vernacular metaphorically, good leaders should look for opportunities to spread the duties among educators and staff so that all will have *a touch* to prove they can lead. This builds a culture of distributive leadership that works magnificently when leaders have trust in their people.

Many schools and districts have a smaller number of go-to people that principals and superintendents always count on. Sort of a star culture. While these stars are to be admired for their dedication and knack for getting things done, we often overutilize them. When this happens, they can become overwhelmed. Better to spread the leadership around and give others an opportunity to shine and show what they can accomplish.

At the point of hiring, a leader should consider leadership potential along with content knowledge. An important role that leaders must play is to build the capacity of their people. This happens when leadership is shared even to the point of stretching people in ways they have never been challenged. When they come through on a leadership charge, they become confident and eager for the next leadership challenge. After a while you have a whole team of leaders!

Rather than wait for volunteers to accept roles, a good leader calls on people. They are flattered, sometimes surprised, and almost always happy to honor the leader's request. Over time a new leader who believes in capacity building eliminates the star culture.

Everyone should get a shot at pulling the heavy leadership wagon. Opportunities for leadership appointments are plentiful. There are program and book adoptions, student behavior committees, assessment work, parent-teacher programming, department chairmanships; the list goes on. Even when people are falling a little short, you can coach them up and help them succeed. In short, you want a culture of leaders on your team!

A FINAL WORD ON BUILDING AND SUSTAINING
A POSITIVE SCHOOL CULTURE

Michael Fullan in his book *Leading in a Culture of Change* (2001) shares the following:

> As educators come under greater pressure to achieve much better and more equitable student outcomes, they will need to leverage every tool available to

them, including organizational culture. Of course, no one suggests that changing culture is simple, easy, or quick. "Reculturing is a contact sport that involves hard, labor-intensive work." But it is a sport that must be played more aggressively if our schools are to achieve the kinds of results we now expect of them. The first step is to help educators recognize that having a strong, positive culture means much more than just safety and order.

As Fullan highlights, changing and sustaining a positive culture is hard work and takes energy. However, it is also very rewarding and fun. What has been outlined in this chapter, while not particularly scholarly, will serve you well as a leader.

SUMMARY QUESTIONS TO PONDER

- In your learning community, does everyone get a chance to lead? Or is there a star system in which only a few are trusted to lead?
- What is the most memorable "little thing" that someone did for you that meant a lot?
- What are the rituals or traditions in your learning community that help define the culture?
- How visible are the leaders of your organization?
- If you are a principal or superintendent, how visible and accessible are you?

Chapter Three

POCDICE

The Processes of Educational Leadership

Keeping up with innovation and change is a leader's biggest challenge. Change should always be focused on how we can get better, how we improve, and how we keep up with educational trends and societal changes.

This is especially true for schools. Best practice, strategy, methods, and technology are constantly evolving. Something new just a couple of years ago can become obsolete very quickly. However, one constant that never changes in school leadership relates to seven critical processes that school leaders must master to be successful.

The late professor emeritus George Chambers from the University of Iowa Educational Leadership Department was a mentor for many principals and superintendents. In his initial foundations of administration class, he would share what were the most important processes of leadership. He identified them as POCDICE. They are as follows:

P—Planning
O—Organization
C—Communication
D—Decision Making
I—Influence/Politics
C—Coordination
E—Evaluation

POCDICE at first sounds like just another stock shelf acronym gimmick. However, as most administrators will attest, a question regarding these processes always comes up in an interview.

"George Chambers was right! As one of his advisees commented almost thirty years later, in every administrative interview I was asked what are the signs of a good leader? Or what are the processes of administration? While I cannot say for sure that my POCDICE response was the determining factor that secured my principal and superintendent jobs, I do remember seeing heads nod as I methodically mentioned each process. I responded the same when posed the same question in interviewing for my current educational leadership position. I continue to pass this on to the principal and superintendent candidates in my classes!"

These processes do not demand that a practitioner has to be a scholar to master them. However, becoming skillful in all of these processes takes time, concentration, and focus. All seven of these processes come into play every day in the life of a principal or administrator.

PLANNING

As a superintendent and principal, certainly being engaged with strategic planning is a common experience in putting in place some long-term planning. This involves establishing a mission, vision, core beliefs, goals, and desired outcomes, but more on this in a later chapter. In this chapter we are looking at planning through the lens of a principal or superintendent in preparation for accomplishing tasks and working with others during a school year.

All planning begins with the calendar. For every school year there are always events with corresponding dates that happen. A good example would be a faculty meeting every second and fourth Tuesday. These events must be placed on the calendar first, thus avoiding scheduling conflicts later. Establishing the end of quarters or terms, parent-teacher conferences, school orientations, registration, Board meetings, and graduation are examples of other events likely to be recurring each year. Once these dates are firmed up, all other scheduling can then proceed. Your goal is to never be surprised by things you should have had planned and on the calendar well in advance.

Things are always going to come up, surprises that might be good or bad. For example, the sudden death of a student or staff member after which counseling plans to support students and members of the learning community may be needed. Or a team qualifies for the state basketball tournament, and you learn the first game the following week is at 11:00 a.m. on Thursday. Such events call for logistics planning and communication.

When planning with others it is important to be open to suggestions and ideas. It is helpful for the leader to begin the meeting with an outline of desired outcomes. This helps kick-start the planning sessions. If delegating the chairmanship of the meeting, ask for an agenda or outline in advance and then get out of the way and let the chair proceed.

The goal of a planning session is to take advantage of the richness that comes out of collaborative discussions in building the best plan possible. Some leaders walk into a meeting without an agenda or outline and try to wing their way to a plan. If a leader invites people to a planning session, there should be evidence of preparation and forethought in passing out an agenda with a timeline in respecting the time of participants.

When it comes to planning, it starts with staying on top of the calendar and looking ahead. While many share responsibilities for scheduling, it is the principal or superintendent with whom the most responsibility resides. The goal is to always anticipate and be prepared!

ORGANIZATION

When it comes to organization, many leaders begin by making lists. One principal shared the following.

"I have always been a Sunday night list maker! I list all the things that I know have to be accomplished in the next week and month, and sometimes even a little further out. This probably sounds sick, but one of my great pleasures in life is crossing out the things on the list after they have been accomplished. For some reason I get great satisfaction in doing this."

As mentioned, the calendar is so important. Be sure you have it up to date and accurate. In the pace of the principalship or superintendency, it is very easy to miss an appointment or meeting if you are not constantly paying close attention to your own daily and weekly calendar. It is embarrassing to miss an appointment or meeting because you did not have it on your calendar or failed to check your schedule closely. Your assistant can help you manage your calendar and time, but you have to take responsibility for being organized and timely per your job performance.

The following are some thoughts related to organization.

Meetings

Only hold a meeting when it is necessary. While in building the calendar a leader might establish a standing faculty meeting. There is nothing wrong in canceling such a meeting if there is not a compelling reason to meet. One of the gestures most appreciated by teachers is getting a notice that a meeting has been canceled! It gives teachers a chance to use this newfound free time productively. In the pace of a busy school year, these standing meetings will normally need to be held. However, canceling a needless meeting for which a memo with announcements will suffice sends a message that you respect the time of others. That does not go unnoticed!

Start and End Meetings on Time

Always start meetings on time! As a new leader, you should indicate up front that meetings will always start and end on time. It would also behoove a new leader to share right from the start your expectations that everyone be punctual.

Have you ever been to a meeting and witnessed people arriving late? Some latecomers actually have the gall to ask the leader, "What did I miss?" as if everyone who arrived on time is not even in the room! This is unprofessional behavior, and a leader should never tolerate this. Demanding punctuality is not an unreasonable expectation. Your staff will get the message when you always start on time.

There may be times that someone arrives late. This can happen to any of us when emergencies and unforeseen things come up. In such cases the latecomer should see the leader at the end of the meeting, explain the tardiness, and find out from a colleague what was missed. A leader should never repeat information for the sake of a latecomer. It sends a poor message to other participants that their time is not valued.

Equally important to starting on time is ending on time. Keep in mind your teachers and staff have other responsibilities, especially at the end of a school day when they have home or child care responsibilities or other calendar obligations they arranged knowing your meeting ending time.

Devices: Put Them Away at Meetings

Along with punctuality being a professional expectation for a meeting, so too should be the silencing and putting away of devices. This includes laptops, phones, and smart watches. The leader needs to stress that attentive listening and professional courtesy for whoever is speaking is something to be honored.

The use of devices can be as distracting as sidebar conversations that disrupt a meeting. Make clear as soon as possible that such behavior is not professional. In beginning a meeting, even a reminder to put away phones is not a bad idea. Movie theaters do it. Many leaders choose to ignore this. The problem festers and grows as more people feel it is okay to check messages and texts. In short, you can demand the professionalism you model at your meetings, and make sure your phone is silenced as well.

Meeting Agenda

Never hold a meeting in which you walk in without an agenda. It is *your meeting.* Prior to the meeting and in establishing your agenda outline, it is a good idea to solicit and invite people to submit topics to be addressed. On receipt of such, they can be included on the agenda, or if time does not allow, on a future agenda if the issue is not pressing. A timeline for agenda items is helpful in staying on task.

Beware of some strong personalities coming into a meeting and right away expressing a concern that is not on the agenda. If not presented to you prior to the meeting, politely acknowledge the concern and indicate it will have to be addressed later. Then quickly get back to the agenda. You will be surprised how people appreciate your running a meeting that allows for discourse but sticks to the agenda and ends on time. Don't ever let anyone hijack your meeting!

On occasion there will be a need for a one-topic agenda or an emergency meeting. These types of meetings should be scheduled only when necessary. Impromptu meetings that are unnecessarily called can really exhaust the energy of a faculty and staff.

Minutes

It's always a good idea to have minutes or notes taken at meetings. It gives the leader an opportunity to follow up and not forget important items and information. A record also helps avoid disagreements or disputes per what was decided at a given time. A leader should have an assistant take minutes and notes and submit them to participants following the meeting. There will be many times you will be thankful that you had a record to look back on.

COMMUNICATION

You can never overcommunicate. It often takes multiple communications for the message you want to convey to resonate with those you lead and work with in your learning community.

One young principal when learning some of his faculty were surprised about an upcoming event lamented, "How can this be, I shared this date in multiple communications and meetings!"

Well, people get busy and are often wrapped up in their own immediate issues whether it be in their classrooms or personal lives. Never assume one communication about something important is ever enough!

Written Communications: Memos, Emails, and Texts

For any important written communication that is high stakes, be sure to have a second set of eyes review it. Your assistant can help you with this, but you might also seek out someone with really strong editing skills. When you are so locked into the message you are crafting, it is easy to overlook grammar and usage mistakes.

There are times one has to wonder if emails and texts are a blessing or a curse. So often tone is misinterpreted, people are reactive rather than thoughtful, and time can be wasted. If there are more than four responses in a thread between two people, a phone call or a face-to-face meeting may be in order. How many times have you seen a thread of messages go on and on? Pretty soon the conversation either deteriorates or becomes more confusing.

Emailing, texting, and electronic messaging are not going away any time soon. Certainly these tools are necessary for us to communicate in a timely manner with an individual or masses of people. However, a high-stakes memorandum or email needs a second set of eyes. Such a practice can eliminate embarrassment, ill feeling, and misunderstanding.

An Economy of Words

The shorter the memo, the more likely people will actually read it. President Reagan would tell his advisors to confine their briefings to one typewritten page. Certainly there are times when detail is warranted. However, how many times have you received a lengthy communication or email that you ignored or skimmed?

Social Media and Websites

In today's world, schools have to be proactive in the use of social media. The information and content must be kept current and monitored. It is critical to have someone with expertise in social media no matter how fiscally strapped a school or district might be. Most districts and schools now have a media specialist in charge of the messaging coming in and going out. Meetings and mailings, while still important and necessary at times, are somewhat a thing of the past. This generation of parents and students check websites for events and news. Thus schools have to provide information where people will look to find it.

Newspaper Articles and Columns

Millennials and those under forty often read their newspapers and articles online. However, senior citizens still like their newspapers and magazines. They also vote at a higher percentage rate than any other group and especially in school district elections.

If you are fortunate enough to live in a town that has a daily or even weekly newspaper, it is foolish not to have a regular presence as a columnist or frequent author of letters to the editor. This keeps all subscribers and especially senior citizens connected with the school system. Without kids in school any longer, the local newspaper is their source for school news. They read Board minutes and follow school expenditures and tax levies the Board of Education approves. For some reason we sometimes forget that empty nesters and senior citizens still want to know what is going on in schools.

One superintendent in a town of twelve thousand people arranged to have a column twice a month in his town's daily paper entitled "Keeping You Informed." The editors and publishers of small town papers are more than happy to print your pieces. It enables them to secure more advertising due to having more copy. Most papers today are shorthanded and grateful for any newsworthy information that appeals to a local community audience.

School news is always of interest per the coverage of athletic teams, plays and musicals, School Board news, posting of honor rolls, and letters to the editor. The local newspaper can often help significantly in securing the senior citizen vote on a referendum, not to mention getting an endorsement from the newspaper and business leaders. It's important to have a positive relationship with the local publisher and reporters.

That Important First Impression

Administrators should pay attention to the setup of their offices. Aside from the desk, there should be a table and chairs. Greeting people and getting out from behind the desk sends a message of comfort and warmth. A business teacher once commented on his first office meeting with a new principal. He recalls knocking on the open door and asking the principal if he could have a word with him.

"Right away the principal got up from behind his desk, greeted me with a handshake, and steered me toward the table and chairs in his office. From that very first greeting, I felt like an equal!"

A major message in this book is the importance of leaders conveying the message of working *with* you. Little things like this make a big difference.

One of the most important presentations an administrator will make is that first time meeting with the faculty and staff all together. Don't begin with the school improvement plan or strategic plan goals. That can wait! Take the time to prepare a very ingratiating presentation.

Include in that talk information about yourself and your family and your interests outside of school. Give them an inside view of the kind of person you are. If you are comfortable telling a humorous story or an interesting past experience, do so! Above all do your homework regarding the learning culture you are inheriting. No matter how dire or distressed a certain school or district is, remember you have staff who have been there for several years, some their whole careers. Find some positives and find out about the rituals and sources of pride. You want to hook them right away. Have them leave that first faculty/staff meeting thinking you will be a leader who will not only be effective but genuine, likeable, and approachable.

When to Open and Close Your Door

Many leaders are fond of saying, "my door is always open." The intent of the message is welcoming, but it can get you into trouble. For sure you want to convey your openness and desire to be accessible and be a good listener. However, at times you must shut your door to either concentrate or meet with someone in private.

Have you ever been in a leader's office having a discussion and the office door is open? People (including assistants) will think nothing of walking in the office and getting the leader's attention about their concerns.

Anytime you agree to meet with someone, you extend courtesy by shutting your office door. In advance, you inform your assistant that except for an emergency, you do not want any interruptions. Shutting the door sends a message to the person that you really want to hear what he or she has to say. This sounds like a little thing, but it means a lot.

Speeches and Presentations

Unless you have great orator skills, never give a speech or public presentation without some backup notes or an outline. Read over your speech and presentation to the point that you almost have it memorized. Unless you are a speech maker like Martin Luther King Jr., Ronald Reagan, or Maya Angelou, have an outline or script to fall back on. If you can deliver a speech in a storytelling fashion, this makes it more real and interesting for your audience. When appropriate, injecting humor and good visuals can keep an audience on message. Dry and wordy PowerPoints are a sure way to lose an audience almost from the start! Typically, the shorter the speeches and presentations, the more likely your message will get through.

Being a Good Listener

The most important communication skill a leader must have is to be a good listener.

Many administrators when reflecting on an issue or event that went poorly can usually attribute this to a lack of attentive listening somewhere in the process. It takes a little more time to get all sides of an issue and to be thorough in planning. However, it is well worth the time spent on the front end. It will save you grief and possible embarrassment in the long run. A leader with good listening skills will almost always have better outcomes.

One final tip on listening. Don't interrupt people. Let people finish what they are saying before you respond. In the fast pace of a school or district, we are often in a hurry to give someone a response before he or she even completes his or her thought. If you have this habit, try to break it. See if you catch yourself with friends or colleagues speaking before they finish a thought. One administrator who had this nasty habit relays how his wife helped him break it.

"We could be driving somewhere and she would be speaking and I would interrupt before she finished her thought. So when I interrupted, she would go stone silent! The silence was a strong signal that 'darn, I did it again!' She would even go silent when we were with friends and family, and I embarrassingly knew I cut in on her and she was angry about it. Gradually I got better in waiting until she completed her thought. It helped me become a better listener not only with her but everyone! Now when others interrupt I recognize just how annoying this habit is!"

Another communication tip you should always keep in mind is when you are greeting people. There was a pastor who was admired for his many wonderful traits. However, he also had a very disturbing habit. He would be greeting an individual after the service with a handshake, but his eyes were gazing elsewhere. This often gave a person the impression that others in the hall were more important. If you are greeting or meeting people in a crowd, they deserve to have their presence affirmed with eye contact and warmth.

One final note about communication. If you are not clear, ask for clarification. It is always wise to make sure you clearly understand what a person has shared with you. You might conclude a conversation by reaffirming what you just heard with this prompt: "If I understand you correctly per what you just shared . . ." It is never good to walk away from a conversation still confused because clarification was not sought.

DECISION MAKING

Decision making is the "D" in the POCDICE axiom. Decisions an administrator makes often determine the destiny of a school or district. Thus a dedicated chapter on decision making will come later in the book. This is such an important process in leadership that it deserves to be discussed as a standalone topic in chapter 9.

INFLUENCE/POLITICS

How many times have you heard an educator, or anyone for that matter, lament, "I hate politics"? Of course in a day and age of special interests, out of control campaign finance, and gerrymandered congressional districts, one does get the feeling that our republic, built on the pillars of democracy and government for all the people, has never been more in jeopardy.

The plight of the poor we readily see in our schools. There are more Title 1 schools and ever increasing numbers of free and reduced lunch eligible students. Herein lies where the leaders of schools always have to be cham-

pions and advocates for equity and opportunity for all students, not just
some! So yes, we have to be influential and at times political.

Influence and having a strong voice are important. When you are the
leader in a learning community, you are under the scrutiny of all who are
impacted by your leadership. Therefore the positions you take and the decisions you make are very important to many people.

Internal and External Influence/Politics

As a principal it is important to have the back of a dedicated and committed
faculty and staff, but not to the point where a principal is not a system player
as well. It's understandable how a principal can feel caught in the middle. In
some school districts new initiatives are adopted every year like the flavor of
the month at an ice cream parlor. This exhausts and frustrates faculty. A
narrow focus per implementing only a couple of major initiatives at a time
will result in better outcomes.

Douglas Reeves in his book *Finding Your Leadership Focus* (2011) addresses initiative fatigue. Principals have to monitor the pulse and pace in
their buildings. They, more than the central office, can see what their teachers can handle and when they are overburdened. Principals have to be proactive in preventing teacher burnout. As Reeves points out, if there are more
than six major initiatives in a given year, the likelihood of success is low.
Even the best people when overwhelmed will lose their focus.

One high school principal was convincing enough to slow down some
district initiatives while implementing a four block schedule. His superiors
listened to him, allowing the four block professional development to be a
singular focus, ensuring successful implementation. Oftentimes central office
people do not realize the climate and level of capacity for change that might
exist in a building. It is the principal's job to communicate passionately and
effectively for his or her learning community.

A principal also needs to advocate for district initiatives that truly advance the learning community, even when teachers in his or her building are
unhappy and resistant. In such cases the principal has to be convincing in
messaging why such a change is important. The Danielson framework is a
good example. Many administrators and teachers are not fans of it being
heavily implemented into evaluation tools. However, there is richness and
value in helping teachers improve their craft through professional development about the four domains. The Danielson framework can also strengthen
the skills of principals as instructional leaders. More on this in the principalship chapter.

In politics there is often a need to find middle ground and compromise.
Tom Loftus served as Speaker of the Assembly in the state of Wisconsin
from 1983 to 1991. In his book *The Art of Legislative Politics* (1994), he

often referenced in his role as speaker the ability to work both sides of the aisle in finding a compromise. "It's better to come home with a half a loaf of bread, than none at all." This applies to school politics as well.

It is also important for school leaders to stand up and embrace issues of social justice. We need to assure that students, families, and staff are treated well in our schools and communities. Take, for example, LGBT and trans-gender policies that have been adopted across our nation; while arrived at with controversy in many communities, these policies protect the rights of those who might otherwise be bullied and harassed. The special education and English language learning student populations have increased. School leaders have to be the champions for populations and causes that need a strong voice. School leaders have an obligation to make sure that everyone feels safe, welcomed, and invited in their learning community.

One final but very important aspect of influence is building coalitions of support. It is a good idea to invite others to assist you in your messaging. Sometimes this means finding people who can get your message across better than you. Take the principal referenced earlier who was implementing a four block schedule in his high school.

"I had a core of teachers who were better at presenting the benefits of the four block than I. From teacher union concerns to more active learning activities, they had the messaging down to a science! I had the passion and spirit and the research behind why this would be a good decision, but the teachers I distributed leadership to, they were more convincing in selling the four block concept!"

COORDINATION

Coordination is the second C in the POCDICE axiom. This is a process that a leader must really pay attention to if a plan is going to be successful.

How many times have you met a really creative and innovative person with great gifts and imagination? Their minds are awesome! While many of these people can see the big picture and provide the coordinates to pull off big ideas, there are some who cannot. For whatever reason, they cannot connect their creativeness with the logistics it takes to bring a plan to fruition.

Very related to planning and organization discussed earlier in this chapter is the attention that must be given to detail and logistics. The good news for any leader is that in a distributive leadership model there is usually someone who is detail oriented. Like a helpful devil's advocate, this person will pains-takingly remind the leader of timelines, preparations, facilities, advance com-munication, and all the little details that if not attended to could derail a plan.

A good example of where coordination can sometimes break down is when a new initiative is brought forward. Often lacking is a well thought out professional development plan with realistic timelines for implementation. Things get rushed often due to political pressure and the initiative fails. This can result in great frustration and often a quick abandonment of what could have been a great initiative had the coordination and planning been better.

Rarely, with a huge initiative, is coordination absolutely perfect. However, if on the front end there has been some good forecasting, planning, and coordination, the likelihood of success, albeit flexible in making changes along the way due to unforeseen circumstances, almost always assures a positive outcome. In short it pays to take a little extra time prior to implementation. This can save a leader a lot of angst and grief later.

EVALUATION

At the risk of overusing the often referred to definition of *insanity* ("doing things over and over and expecting different results"), the process of evaluation is critically important for a leader. Evaluation being referred to here (not to be confused with teacher/staff evaluation to be discussed later) is the continuous review of programming, practices, and initiatives to assure they remain effective in meeting desired outcomes. Over time changes, modification, tweaks, and even abandonment may be necessary.

As leaders we get invested in ideas we really like and programs we have played a big part in designing and bringing forward. One of the biggest traps in leadership is to let your pride get in the way of a needed change. In short we can get stubborn; thus abandonment becomes difficult for us.

Earlier it was noted that active listening is the most critical communication skill. It really comes into play in evaluation. How open are we to diverse thoughts and opinions when evaluating a program or making a needed change? Sometimes we want to "kill our messenger," but the messenger is indeed the person who can save us from our own ego. Good leaders encourage advisors and leadership team members to be candid and straightforward. They embrace a team spirit. We all benefit from honest evaluation in making good decisions.

One principal related an example of her stubbornness.

"We implemented a silent sustained reading program in the nineties at my high school. I thought it was a great idea and so did my allies in language arts and on the library faculty! How often do we hear students need to read more? Students and staff alike could bring in their favorite books or reading materials. School texts were not included. We adjusted the seven-period schedule every Wednesday. For a half hour at 10:00 a.m. students and staff would read for thirty minutes, nothing else could take place. Many found it enjoyable and a peaceful break in what otherwise could be a hectic schedule.

"Well, some students would come in without reading materials, so we had extra reading materials on hand including all kinds of magazines including Sports Illustrated, Newsweek, Time *magazine, and all kinds of books that might appeal to high school students. I remember one junior boy facetiously asking me if I could have some* Playboy *magazines on hand. I gave him my best stink eye and he got the message!*

"Well it took six months for me to be convinced that maybe we should abandon the idea. This despite the pleas of my assistant principals and even my allies, complaining that discipline issues and noncompliance were just too overwhelming! Many on my staff began to dread Wednesdays, but not me! I loved reading so I was really reluctant to deem this initiative unsuccessful. I thought in time things would get better. In hindsight I should have ended the program after a month. The disruption trumped the benefits. Even to this day I think it was a good idea. I have a hard time letting go of my stubbornness."

A closing thought on evaluation. It never hurts to try new things. However, we also have to have the gumption to abandon things that are not meeting our desired outcomes. We have to be honest and open in our evaluations in welcoming collaborative points of view in making prudent decisions that are good for the learning community.

In summarizing this chapter, mastering POCDICE and understanding the importance of focusing on these processes of leadership will serve aspiring and current practicing leaders well. These processes provide the underpinning for a healthy culture. Moreover, they assure that we will provide programs and services that will allow our children and our youth to reach their academic and personal potential.

SUMMARY QUESTIONS TO PONDER

- Of the POCDICE processes, what are your strengths as a leader, and what would be the areas you would need to work on improving?
- Are you a good listener, or do you interrupt before a person has finished speaking?
- Do you plan and organize your meetings well? Do you start them and finish them on time?
- How influential are you when needing to convince others to support important decisions or initiatives?

Part II

Leadership: At the Building Level

Chapter Four

The Principalship

Instructional Leader or Manager?

In this chapter we will take a look at the role of the principal. In earlier chapters we covered a lot of ground related to culture and leadership processes (POCDICE). In this chapter we will take a look at the principalship role as both an instructional leader and a manager. The principal, more than anyone, determines if a school will flourish. As time goes on, the job continues to evolve and become more complex.

In the past twenty years there has been a great emphasis on the principal being the instructional leader versus a manager. A confluence of both roles seems to be the order of the day when reviewing postings for principal vacancies.

The principal sets the tone for the building. The most important role of a principal is determining who will be on the educational team. No other evaluation is more important than who is hired and who is retained. This more than anything else will define the culture of a learning community.

Building a great faculty and staff is the number one job of a principal. Like in the NFL, you must draft well, find some good free agents, and continuously be committed to player development in assuring your teachers and staff continually grow and build their capacity. As mentioned in an earlier chapter, you want to develop a building of leaders. Content knowledge is important, but you also need people who can grow into leaders.

Can a principal be both an instructional leader and a manager? The answer to this question better be yes if you hope to be hired these days. However, it has been a disservice to the profession in recent years to see the role of manager downplayed in the literature almost as if it were a negative attribute.

Rarely are principals dismissed due to lacking instructional leadership. It is on the management end where principals get fired. It could be a misuse of funds, communication and relationship issues, negligence related to safety measures, or poor decisions impacting students, staff, or the community unrelated to instructional processes.

The really great principals are also great managers. In fact, there are many great principals who understand their greatest weakness is in instructional leadership. They may not feel very comfortable in curricular programming, assessment, and data-driven decision making. However, they understand that academic growth and continual improvement are the benchmarks of instructional excellence. These principals surround themselves with others who can help them build a strong academic agenda. They delegate to those who can connect with others in the planning and implementation of important instructional decisions.

As a manager, a principal works tirelessly to provide everything possible for teachers and staff to succeed. This includes assuring facilities are safe and clean and providing necessary resources, equipment, and technology. Teachers also value knowing that their principal has their back. For all of this to happen, a principal must have strong management skills.

Another important management skill is an ability to anticipate and forecast. A principal with good management skills is out ahead of things. In short, the faculty and staff are rarely ever surprised by an occurrence. This is especially important with emergency plans. Like NASA, "you will perform the way you have drilled." A good principal/manager has people prepared.

In table 4.1 Glathom, Boschee, and Whitehead (2006) addressed principal leadership responsibilities as they relate to instructional and curricular leadership. Without a doubt, any principal demonstrating excellence in all of these performance responsibilities would be considered outstanding. Read these carefully!

As you review each of these important responsibilities, most would be classified as management/culture building skills rather than instructional leadership. It is critically important that the principal accepts great responsibility for advancing the academic agenda and goals of the school. However, many outstanding principals are not well versed in all curricular disciplines, instructional pedagogy, and assessment.

Great principals have well-honed skills in distributive leadership. While not abrogating responsibility, they understand that delegating instructional leadership to others can advance the learning community. The good news is that the principal can enlist the help of others in building capacity and maintaining a strong instructional focus in a building.

Table 4.1. Principal Leadership Responsibilities

Responsibilities	*The extent to which the principal . . .*
Culture	establishes a set of standard operating procedures and routines.
Discipline	protects teachers from issues and influences that would detract from their teaching time and focus.
Resources	provides teachers with materials and professional development necessary for the successful execution of their roles.
Curriculum, Instruction, Assessment	is directly involved in the design and implementation of curriculum, instruction, and assessment practices.
Focus	establishes clear goals and keeps those goals at the forefront of the school's attention.
Knowledge of Curriculum, Instruction, Assessment	is knowledgeable about current curriculum, instruction, and assessment practices.
Contingent Rewards	recognizes and rewards individual accomplishments.
Communication	establishes strong lines of communication with teachers and students.
Outreach	is an advocate and spokesman for the school to all stakeholders.
Input	demonstrates an awareness of the personal aspects of teachers and staff.
Affirmation	recognizes and celebrates school accomplishments and acknowledges failure.
Relationship	demonstrates an awareness of the personal aspects of teachers and staff.
Change Agent	is willing to and actively challenges the status quo.
Optimizer	inspires and leads new and challenging innovations.
Ideals/Beliefs	communicates and operates from strong ideals and beliefs about schooling.
Monitors/Evaluates	monitors the effectiveness of school practices and their impact on student learning.
Flexibility	adapts leadership behavior to the needs of the current situation and is comfortable with dissent.
Situational Awareness	is aware of the details and undercurrents in the running of the school and uses this information to address current and potential problems.
Intellectual Stimulation	ensures the faculty and staff are aware of the most current theories and practices and makes the discussion of these a regular aspect of the school's culture.

ELEMENTARY PRINCIPALS

Many elementary principals, most notably in schools with five hundred students or fewer, do not have an assistant principal. They are expected to evaluate their teachers and staff and provide instructional leadership along with managing the building. In such learning communities, relying on teacher leaders is a must. Even in a small elementary school it is hard for a principal to lead instruction and manage the building without significant help from teachers and staff.

MIDDLE SCHOOL PRINCIPALS

Middle school–level buildings or intermediate buildings are typically grades 5 through 8, serving students ten to fourteen years of age. There still remain some junior high structures (grades 7, 8, and sometimes 9). What is somewhat fascinating to ponder is that districts rarely design a middle school or junior high. There are many middle school buildings in the United States that were formerly high school facilities. Often communities will opt to build a new high school, thus a building designed for high school–aged students may lack that affective and warm environmental feeling needed for ten to fourteen year olds!

Most middle schools have larger enrollments than the elementary buildings that feed into them. The shift to middle schools from junior highs began in the sixties. The shift to a more sensitive, affective approach to children transitioning to adolescence was an important consideration, with houses made up of interdisciplinary teams of teachers in core subjects along with elective exploratory cycles in which students have six weeks for foreign language, technology, and family and consumer education, along with taking art, physical education, and music.

Most middle school principals have an assistant principal if the enrollment exceeds five hundred students. House leaders and department heads are delegated leadership by the principal for both instructional and managerial tasks.

HIGH SCHOOL PRINCIPALS

High schools like middle schools usually have larger enrollments and assistant principals assigned to assist the principal. Principals in high schools with 350 to 3,500 students enrolled (or more), in addition to having assistant principals, rely on department heads for instructional, managerial, and more recently evaluation responsibilities.

One suburban high school principal with an enrollment of three thousand students was quoted as stating, "This school is like a little city, with neighborhoods, streets, unique challenges, and a culture of its own. Thank God, I have good people I can delegate to in helping me run this place."

In recapping this chapter, instructional leadership and managerial leadership are both important for a building principal. Whether the school is small or large, principals must have a distributive leadership plan in place to move forward in having a safe, welcoming, and instructionally progressive learning community.

SUMMARY QUESTIONS TO PONDER

- Per the Glathorn, Boshee, Whitehead chart indicating principal leadership responsibilities, which are your strengths? Which are areas you would need to improve on?
- What do you feel are the strongest managerial attributes a principal must possess?
- What are indications to you that a principal is a strong instructional leader?
- If a principal is not invested, can a school still have a positive culture?

Chapter Five

Hiring Great People

From Recruitment to Induction

You can't make a good apple pie if you have bad apples! The same is true in building a great faculty and staff. Oftentimes principals rush into hiring only to regret it later. Hiring has to be a very thoughtful process. A principal must determine if the candidate has the qualifications, credentials, and skills to improve the faculty team. It sounds simple but it takes some great preparation and diligence to hire the best candidate.

The first important step is the posting of the position. Great care should be given to how the posting is written. It should indicate exactly what a principal wants per meeting the school's needs in filling the vacancy. A thorough and complete job description should also be developed that clearly specifies expectations.

Usually human resources departments and collective bargaining agreements will define posting timelines and steps to be followed. However, some principals get lazy and will automatically hire an internal candidate because a transfer might not be as cumbersome. Internal candidates may well be highly qualified and the best choice. However, like all other applicants they should be required to prove themselves among all the internal and external candidates. Such decisions can be very difficult for a principal, who may have to deal with some hard feelings. It is never easy to pass over a strong internal candidate, but a principal has the obligation to be objective in hiring the best candidate.

Anytime you hire someone it is with the idea that you will be improving the position and the learning community. One might challenge this premise given the many great teachers who may be retiring. When hiring, the principal should look beyond a candidate's current credentials and skills. Moreover, the principal should also try to discern the capacity for growth and leadership the candidate may possess. At times it is also helpful to build a profile of traits and skills you desire in a new hire. Soliciting input from teachers and staff who will work closely with the new hire can be very insightful as well.

SCREENING APPLICATIONS AND CANDIDATE PAPERS

There are no shortcuts to this process. When you invite people to apply for a position in your school, you owe it to them to read and review their papers carefully. The only exception would be if you discovered right away the candidate was not certified for the position as the posting clearly stated. Many principals might ask department chairs or grade level teachers to review some files to gather additional insight from another set of eyes. Winnowing down excellent candidates to ten is a good target, with the goal of eventually bringing in five candidates for interviews after background checks and reference calls.

Background and social media checks are essential in the screening process. Many school districts have been embarrassed to learn that new hires have criminal offenses or social media posts that disqualify them from working in a school setting. In such cases the trust in leadership is greatly marginalized and the negative publicity is hard to overcome. Contracts have to be rescinded. Some administrators have lost their jobs due to their carelessness in not putting forth due diligence in the screening process.

SCOUTING REPORTS

The greatest predictor of how a candidate will perform is his or her past performance record. Again this is an area that a principal should spend considerable time in checking references. In addition to references noted on a candidate's résumé, a principal should also touch base with past supervisors who might not be listed. It pays to get as many references as possible.

The phone call almost always reveals more than the letter in a candidate's file. Some human resources departments forbid sharing any information other than the starting and ending date of employment. A principal who runs up against this has to press on and find a way to speak with others in the district.

In making reference calls, the principal should develop a script of questions to ask. A good last question is, "If you had an opportunity would you hire this person again?" The answer can give you some valuable insight. As a rule, never eliminate a candidate because of one bad reference among several more glowing reports. Personality conflicts happen, and as the saying goes, reading the tea leaves comes into play.

When hiring teachers just beginning their careers, the key reference is the cooperating teacher. Again, the phone call will reveal more than the recommendation letter if some thought has been put into questions to ask. Speaking with the building principal can be helpful, but typically he or she has not observed the student teacher unless he or she anticipated an opening in his or her own building. This is mostly due to the heavy teacher evaluation load he or she already has. University supervising teachers can be helpful as well, but it is the cooperating teacher who will know your potential hire best.

INTERVIEWING CANDIDATES

Some principals and districts will hold preliminary interviews first before final interviews or even doing reference calls. The face-to-face preliminary interview conducted by the principal can help winnow down the list of final candidates.

Typically, a principal will include teachers, assistant principals, staff, parents, and sometimes students in an interview process. It seems a waste of time to hold an interview and not be able to share a scouting report with them on the candidates. After all, they are giving up the better part of a day to assist in interviews. Many people can interview well and fool interview teams per the stilted conversations that might take place for an hour. This is why the scouting report is so important. It is good to share at the end of the interviews.

In scheduling interviews, like a sporting tournament, one principal liked to seed the candidates one through five, having the top seed based on the references and scouting reports leading off. In his opinion, this set the bar for the second seed and others to follow. Ideally, it would be difficult to choose among the top seeds based on the quality of the candidate pool.

The questions asked should be targeted and meaningful. At the end of the interview, the principal and the interview team should have a clear idea of whether a candidate is a good match for the need. Scripted questions should be prepared. It is important that all candidates answer the same questions. The principal needs to advise this protocol in advance so interview team members do not stray.

In many interviews today, a candidate, in addition to answering questions, might be asked to present a lesson or demonstrate critical thinking skills in a basket exercise. The latter gives the principal an indication of the writing skills of a candidate and how he or she might handle a difficult issue.

THE HIRING DECISION RESTS WITH THE PRINCIPAL

In some hiring situations, a vote is taken after all interviews are completed and the winner is democratically chosen. Again, this is sometimes done even prior to a background and scouting report being completed. This type of process has many flaws.

Who will be responsible for the new hire's performance? Of course it is the principal's role to induct, observe, coach, mentor, and evaluate the new hire. It is the role of the principal to help the new hire transition into the learning community culture.

For these reasons, the principal should make it clear to an interview team right from the start that input is invited and welcomed but the final decision will rest with the principal. Most interview teams will feel relieved to know this and still feel affirmed that their principal desired their input and included them in the process.

In the best hiring processes, the principal will have great angst in deciding the best candidate to choose. This is because of the extensive preparation and work done on the front end in recruiting and vetting excellent candidates for the position.

Once the candidate is chosen, a call offering the position should be made immediately. Hopefully the chosen candidate will accept right away. However, there are times when candidates will ask for more time. Chances are they have been on the radar of other schools and districts who, like you, recruited them. Depending on circumstances, twenty-four hours or a weekend at the most should be tops. In the event the person declines, you want time to offer the position to your runner-up candidate, and maybe even the third choice!

On confirmation that you have a candidate hired, contact by phone all those who you interviewed. Inform them of the decision and thank them as well for interviewing with you and preparing their papers. To be sure the unsuccessful candidates will feel some disappointment. Keep them in mind as your paths may cross again! You want to be remembered as respectful and classy even in this difficult conversation.

One final observation related to hiring: a short thank you note should be sent to all applicants regarding the final decision. Have you ever wondered about a job you applied for and if a decision has been made? You want to call but are fearful of appearing pushy or sounding desperate. An applicant who has been asked to complete an application and prepare accompanying papers deserves a response in a reasonable amount of time regarding the hiring decision. While it may leave the applicant disappointed in not being selected, a gracious response lets the candidate move on, appreciating your professionalism in getting back to him or her.

THE IMPORTANCE OF INDUCTION

The most important period of time for new teachers out of college is the first six weeks. As capable and competent as they may be in their discipline, they usually need guidance and mentorship, especially when it comes to classroom management. A good mentor teacher should be assigned to a new teacher. It is helpful for the new teacher to meet with the mentor for a few minutes each day and for an hour every week of the first semester. Ideally a strong relationship and bond will form and new teachers will feel comfortable approaching their mentors with questions and concerns they may have as they begin their careers.

The principal and the assistant should also drop by the new teacher's classroom before and after school frequently to build rapport and provide encouragement. Aside from the observations and evaluations, the new teachers have to feel supported by their leaders.

When hiring an experienced teacher, mentorship is still important. The cultural difference from one building or district to another can seem like night and day. While the mentorship does not need to be as intense for a veteran joining a new staff, there should be a plan in place. Principals and assistants again should stop by frequently in offering their help and support.

In closing out this chapter, the induction process is the often forgotten element in the hiring process after recruitment and selection has taken place. We owe it to the people we bring into our learning communities to really help them make a successful transition. It is sad when young people leave our profession. Often this can be traced to a lack of support at the beginning of their teaching careers. Mentorship and support in a good induction process are an investment that the best principals and leaders provide in selecting and keeping good teachers.

SUMMARY QUESTIONS TO PONDER

- Do you have an induction program in place for new teachers that is year-round?
- What supports are in place for new hires?
- Are reference and background checks done after or before candidates are brought in for interviews?
- Are first-year teachers supported with mentoring and professional development that help them with class management and other first-year teaching challenges?

Chapter Six

Selecting and Developing Assistant Principals

One of the greatest joys principals can experience is when one of their loyal assistants moves on to accept a first principalship. Like in the NFL, when an assistant, maybe an offensive or defensive coordinator, moves on to a first head coaching job! You take pride in the people you select as assistants. They helped you significantly in leading your learning community. You helped them grow in their leadership. Now they have an opportunity!

Where principals have assistant principals, it is understood the job is just too big and complex for one person. An assistant is someone a principal not only develops and mentors but also allows to share ideas and even challenge the principal in crucial conversations. Spirited conversations are often the order of the day when a principal and assistants meet to review matters. Principals need to be good listeners. It is also helpful for them to have someone to confide in and even vent to on occasion. The trademark of a strong administrative team in a building is an unshakable trust and faith in each other.

Some principals really do a disservice to their assistants. They design job descriptions that are almost totally dealing with discipline and redirecting student behavior. Hall supervision, lunch duty, and bus duty, while important, are intellectually dull if not mixed in with some fun and exciting responsibilities.

A good principal will delegate both instructional and management responsibilities to assistants. Activities like National Honor Society, Student Senate, working with department chairs, scheduling, mentoring young teachers, summer school leadership, budget monitoring in some areas, evaluation responsibilities for certified and noncertified staff, leading program adoptions, or text selections are examples of duties that help assistant principals grow.

There are some assistant principals who are very good at their roles and have no desire to become a principal. They become career assistants and are sometimes the stability link that helps keep a school culture from deteriorating due to constant turnover. They enjoy being in the assistant role and are loyal to the principal(s) they serve. They continue to grow in their role because of their own special intrinsic motivation.

For most assistant principals, the learning curve is two to four years. After that they can become very complacent, especially if their role had been mostly as a disciplinarian. This is why it is so important to diversify and give assistants challenging roles that will stimulate them intellectually and build their confidence. As one principal shared, "I want assistants who have a fire in their belly and are willing to take on tasks that will prepare them to move on to their own show."

SELECTING ASSISTANT PRINCIPALS

When putting together an administrative team, a principal must think strategically. The temptation may be strong to select friends and associates who you like or who share a common philosophy. This could be a big mistake. At times principals hire former colleagues and friends. Certainly this can work out well given the trust and loyalty that has been built up. However, if things start to go sour, then both a professional and personal relationship are lost.

A principal really has to examine the needs of the learning community. A soul-searching self-evaluation is needed as well. Ideally a principal would select an assistant candidate who might have strengths the principal does not. Perspectives that can truly broaden the administrative reach in addressing learning community needs and challenges cannot be underestimated.

In all schools it can be a great asset to a principal to have assistants who are persons of color. Regardless of your opinion of the white privilege premise, a look at things from a different lens can be enlightening and fruitful in creating a culture of sensitivity. We often hear of the good old boy's network, in which male principals hire other men to be on their teams. Gender diversity whether you are a male or female principal is something you should consider seriously. One urban high school principal with twenty-two hundred pupils recalled hiring a woman assistant because of her reputation as an outstanding master scheduler. He later shared, "She brought a lot more than her scheduling skills, her perspective on issues made us think about things differently and more deliberately. She made our leadership team better!"

SMALL SCHOOLS AND TEACHER LEADERSHIP TEAMS

In metro areas you have large high schools, middle schools, and elementary schools. With large enrollments the principal and assistant principals are commonplace. However, most districts in our country are small towns and rural districts. In these schools there is only one principal. Like larger schools, instructional expectations are high! Parents and families expect their children to receive an outstanding education in a safe, clean, and orderly environment.

In smaller schools there is a great need for the principal to develop and grow teacher leaders. These leaders can help in many ways instructionally and culturally. A distributive leadership approach that empowers teachers and staff is needed to carry out plans and lead initiatives in small schools. There often exists a personalized approach and philosophy that parents and families find very appealing in choosing to live in a small town. Principals in these communities are wise to utilize the talents of teachers and staff.

In summary, principals have a great responsibility to select outstanding assistant principals and help them grow in their skills. This can best be done by diversifying their job descriptions with meaningful tasks that are challenging and important in advancing the learning community. In small schools where the principal is the only administrator in the building, trusting faculty and staff to help lead instructional and management initiatives encourages ownership and pride in the school community.

SUMMARY QUESTIONS TO PONDER

- Does your administrative team include people of color and different genders?
- What responsibilities do your assistants have in their job descriptions? Is there a challenge beyond redirecting student behavior?
- What responsibilities and roles do you as principal feel comfortable assigning to your assistant principals?
- If you are a candidate for an assistant principal position, what roles would you like to have in assisting the principal on an administrative team?

Chapter Seven

Teacher Evaluation

A Reflective Look at Current Practice

Since the seventies a lot of attention and research has gone into the best practices related to teacher evaluation. The most important evaluation is when we hire. After hiring, how do we continue to assist teachers in growing professionally and continuously improving their craft?

A priest who was principal in a Catholic high school in the Midwest was once asked by a young dean of students working on his principal certification why he didn't observe and evaluate teachers. The priest answered, "I know who the good teachers are merely by walking by their classroom." Well for sure this was probably an oversimplified response by the good Father, but in many ways perhaps true!

Over the years, the works of Madeline Hunter, Robert Marzano, Doug Reeves, John Goodlad, Ron Edmonds, Larry Lezotte, Brian McNulty, and many others have established that leadership makes a difference in student achievement.

Some of the finest research of late has been the work of Charlotte Danielson. Her framework is succinct and easy to follow in advancing teaching and learning. It has brought focus to planning and preparation and creating an environment of respect and rapport. It also encourages engaging classroom practice while bringing clarity regarding the most important teacher responsibilities.

Along with the Danielson research, the emergence of academic coaches in the past fifteen years has really had a positive impact on improving instruction. This coaching began with elementary teachers in the areas of literacy and mathematics. We now have coaches in science, social studies, STEM studies, and at all grade levels through high school. The best thing about a

49

coaching model is that it is nonthreatening. Thus teachers receiving the coaching are more receptive as they do not view the coaching as a punitive measure. Moreover, they see it as a way they can really get better.

A thunder cloud on the horizon is the accountability movement and the pressure that has been placed on principals to do walkthroughs and observations. While principal observations are extremely important, the Danielson Framework is often used in an almost robotic, punitive manner.

Most principals today will tell you they are running on empty given the caseload of evaluations they must complete in a year. The Danielson Framework now, built into evaluation tools and used subjectively, leaves many outstanding teachers feeling great angst about the ratings they might receive. In Illinois they are rated (1) Unsatisfactory, (2) Needs Improvement, (3) Proficient, and (4) Excellent.

It's pretty easy to identify teachers doing a poor job of teaching. They are deserving of a rating of 1 for unsatisfactory performance. These teachers need a well thought out growth plan addressing their deficiencies. The principal provides assistance and a professional development plan to assist the teacher in addressing the deficiencies. A timeline for reviewing the growth plan is established. At this point a decision has to be made to either retain or nonrenew the teacher. Confronting and nonrenewing a subpar teacher is not a pleasant thing. However, a principal has an obligation to hire and retain teachers who are worthy of being part of the learning community faculty.

Where the Danielson evaluation tool gets into trouble is in determining whether a teacher is a two or a three or a three or a four. Is he or she proficient or excellent? The numerical rating can really be subjective and can result in a teacher feeling great anxiety. Especially when a dedicated, hardworking teacher believes he or she should be rated as a four but receives a three rating.

The same is true for a teacher who feels he or she is proficient and receives a two (needs improvement). The self-esteem and morale of a teacher can be a delicate thing and far too important to split hairs over a subjective numerical rating. Most beginning teachers need three to five years to become what one instructional coach referred to as "an emerging competent." An important role of a good principal that cannot be dismissed or taken lightly is the ability to build confidence in teachers, and especially young ones. Patience and encouragement on the part of the principal are far more effective than a numerical rating.

This misuse of the framework is very similar to the manipulation of the Madeline Hunter work in the eighties. Her seven-step lesson design was intended to be instructive to teachers in improving their lesson design. However, it was embedded into evaluation documents and viewed punitively. The lament of many teachers back then was, "We have been Hunterized."

Until the end of time evaluation processes and tools will be criticized and never deemed perfect. However, manipulating coaching models into evaluative tools is not the answer in building teacher capacity. Furthermore, the energy of principals is being exhausted. Their overloaded caseloads have resulted in less impactful evaluations. For teachers, far more benefit would be found in collaboration and peer time to review curriculum, make data-driven decisions in reviewing common assessments, and in working together in professional learning communities.

A principal that can build leadership teams and distribute leadership to teacher leaders has a much better chance of establishing a culture of continuous growth in a faculty. Finding time for collaboration would be the key. Allowing teachers to discuss and review best teaching practices and assessment tools would be a far better use of time than the frantic observation cycles that have little impact in improving instruction. As Fullan (2014) notes, "when the principal assumes the role of lead learner and creates a collaborative culture in which practice and pedagogy are linked to results, teachers accept ownership and sustained progress and improvement becomes a cornerstone of the culture."

Fullan (2014) addresses some of the really unintended negative consequences that have come about as a result of the accountability era and the time demands now made on principals. Their time is eaten up with mandatory policies that demand they do classroom observations, often with a checklist. When talking to many teachers, they oftentimes complain that they hear nothing regarding the principal having stopped in. Or if they get some feedback it is shallow and not very helpful.

Rather than spend so much time on walkthroughs and drop-ins, Fullan suggests investing time in building capacity in people. Finding more collaborative time and investing in people's skills will render greater accountability if people are committed to results, to their peers, and to the building or system as a whole.

As Fullan states per improved results in Ontario, "We have accomplished widespread improvement in literacy and high school graduation across the entire public school system of forty-nine hundred schools and seventy-two districts. We have no overt accountability beyond high expectations, investing in capacity building, increasing transparency of results and practice, and maintaining a relentless focus on progress."

It's time to take a step back and review the breakneck pace that principals are currently trying to maintain. Would this time be better allocated to creating collaborative professional learning communities to review data and focus on pedagogy, results, and peer sharing? Wouldn't this also encourage teachers to take more ownership and accept accountability for progress and school and district improvement? Systemic cohesiveness and the principal as the lead learner could foster this all-in culture if given time and not interfered with by legislatures and reactionary School Boards.

Before leaving this area, teacher observations and evaluations are important. However, for veteran teachers who have proven they are good teachers, an annual evaluation is not necessary. Moreover, principals need more time to work with new or struggling teachers in the evaluation process. When teachers have the time to collaborate and work together, they grow and become better professional educators. When time is reallocated to build a collaborative culture focused on pedagogy and results, accountability for improved teaching and learning will be more readily accepted by those who have the most direct contact with our learners—our teachers!

SUMMARY QUESTIONS TO PONDER

• Do your instructional coaches support classroom teachers in building their capacity?
• How much time does your school invest in building teacher capacity?
• Is your evaluation system effective in helping teachers grow?

Chapter Eight

The Importance of Support Staff, Visibility, and Supervision in a Building

In this short chapter, the role of the support staff, visibility, and supervision in a learning community needs to be discussed.

Invariably a strong learning community has a strong support staff. In many communities the school district is the largest employer in the town. Many of the employees are noncertified, and without their roles and contributions, principals and teachers could not do their jobs.

It is important that the principal embraces noncertified staff as important members of the team. Furthermore, it is important for the principal to make sure the faculty respects and honors these staff members as well. Just like teachers, good support staff members take great pride in their work. From the receptionist who greets people cheerfully to the custodian who has floors cleaned and waxed beautifully at the start of every year, the principal sets the tone in affirming these people. Just as we have celebrations to affirm and recognize teachers and students, there should be times during the school year when we include and recognize support staff in celebrations.

Just as for teachers, the principal has to have high expectations for the support staff. A principal should never tolerate a dirty building or a grouchy clerk or secretary. The principal must demand the very best of support personnel; anything less is not acceptable.

A unique relationship is the role of the administrative assistant to the principal. We no longer refer to these roles as secretaries. They are assistants and they can either be a great asset or a detriment to a principal if expectations are not made clear at the start.

A principal when first hired should set aside some purposeful time with his or her new assistant. These initial conversations are most successful when the principal takes the time to prepare an outline with job expectations. It is also important for the new principal to be a good listener in these conversations in getting to know what would be helpful to the assistant. There are some horror stories in which the assistant who perhaps served in the position for many years thinks he or she can dictate to the new principal how the school is to be run. One new principal overheard the assistant commenting to a teacher that "this is the fourth principal I will be breaking in." Well, that just isn't the way it should work!

The most important nonnegotiable is attitude. This, of course, is true for every adult in a learning community. However, the receptionist and your assistant are the voices and faces of the building when people call in or come to the office. It is important that all the clerical staff in the office and the assistant are viewed as pleasant and helpful in receiving people.

An assistant can be most helpful when the principal shares daily and weekly plans keeping the assistant informed. A new principal should provide an induction and orientation process that is so good that eventually the assistant and the principal are in sync with office practices. In the final analysis, the most important aspect of the principal-assistant relationship is *trust*. There are many confidential matters that an assistant will be aware of that must remain under wraps. There can be no gossip or slips of the tongue about serious matters pertaining to the office of the principal.

Custodians are also key support staff players. The principal must demand that the building is safe and clean. Daily and frequent communication in building a relationship with the custodial staff is not stressed nearly enough in college and university educational administration programs. The building and grounds and maintenance of a facility are key managerial responsibilities that a principal must supervise. The relationship, especially with the head custodian, is important. It is something that the rest of the faculty and staff should be able to readily observe, knowing they too need to be respectful and thankful for the good work a custodial staff puts forth. They are an important part of the team!

In short the principal sets the tone in making sure that everyone understands that the noncertified staff is critical to the success of a school. As such they should be valued and affirmed for the great work they do.

VISIBILITY, ACCESSIBILITY, AND SUPERVISION

A healthy culture in a learning community has high expectations for respectful behavior. It is important to review behavior plans and conduct codes so that expectations are clearly understood by the students, faculty, and staff.

Student handbooks and codes of conduct are an extension of Board policy, so changes made annually should be approved by the Board of Education prior to the start of a school year.

Most buildings have what might be referred to as "hot spots." Typically, these are near entrances, commons areas, hallway intersections, playgrounds, bus pickup spots, and parking lots. The best preventative measure is adult supervision. It should be noted that the majority of the time these are gathering places where happy exchanges are taking place. Thus it is good for a principal to frequent these spots and greet students.

One high school principal noted that if she stood at one large hall intersection at 7:55 a.m., she would likely see and greet three-fourths of her student body as they moved from the commons to their first hour class. This allowed students to ask her questions and express concerns because she was *accessible.* She noted, "Some of the concerns students shared were things that would have never been brought to my office."

Students are going to have issues. A fight or argument is less likely to occur if there is a well thought out supervision plan. One urban principal implored teachers to help him and his three assistant principals with supervision. Prior to his arrival, fights took place frequently along with gang activity. During passing times in this four-hundred-thousand-square-foot high school, teachers remained in their rooms during the five-minute interval. There were hall monitors, but not nearly enough to see everything. With four floors and one hundred and fifty teachers, the principal shared that "when you stand by your room door during passing time, we have an adult in place every twenty-five feet. Help me make this school safe and less violent."

His faculty responded, and mostly because they saw his visibility and relentless efforts to get the school under control. As a result, fights, disruptive behavior, and discipline referrals were dramatically reduced. The morale and culture of the school improved, as did its reputation as an urban high school to emulate.

There has to be structure and high expectations for student behavior. A principal and the assistant principals cannot do it alone. The principal who stays in the office and is not visible cannot expect teachers and staff to be actively involved in supervision. Even assistant principals who are assigned supervision will do so with less enthusiasm when their leader is not visible.

It takes a team effort of adults in a building invested and committed to making sure a school is safe and welcoming. When teachers and staff are visible along with the principal and assistants, student behavior will always be vastly improved. Adult supervision matters, and when the principal is out front and visible, the rest of the staff will follow when asked to help with supervision.

In closing out this chapter, it takes a team to establish high expectations for learning and student behavior. A good principal is visible and accessible to the students and staff during a school day. Getting out of the office, knowing where the hot spots are, and informally communicating with students, faculty, staff, and parents are great ways to build relationships!

SUMMARY QUESTIONS TO PONDER

- Is the support staff student friendly in your school?
- How are people received in your building or district when they come into the office or contact the building or district by phone?
- Are the principal, superintendent, and leaders in the building or district visible and accessible for students, faculty, staff, and parents?
- Do the adults in the building help others feel safe, welcomed, and invited into the learning community?

Chapter Nine

Decision Making

When the Tough Ones Come Your Way

The decisions leaders make often define how they will be remembered. There has never existed a leader who made only *right decisions*. We live and we learn. Many books have been written by thought leaders and industry giants on decision making. Being deliberate in gathering all the information needed before arriving at a decision is the best approach.

Peter Drucker, a management consultant, author, and educator, designed a six-step decision-making model that if followed closely minimizes the likelihood of making a poor decision.

DRUCKER SIX-STEP DECISION-MAKING MODEL

Step 1: Problem Clarification

Is the problem generic or unique? If the problem is generic or something that has occurred before, then there is a precedence, policy, or handbook procedure on how to resolve the problem. If the problem is unique, then a reliance on principles and judgment come into play. As an example, the appropriate use of technology is an area where something unique comes up just about every year. A new issue! This results in school leaders needing to make decisions for which there is no precedence or policy. Eventually because of the experience, a policy and handbook revision will come later.

Step 2: Problem Definition

This step calls for a thorough look at a situation in reviewing all the issues. This is where we often miss the mark. In our fast-paced roles, we often fail to adequately define the issue or problem. In short, we reactively try to resolve the problem without having all the information we need. When this happens, we often get a poor outcome and as a result we have to start over.

A trap one young administrator fell into in his early years as a principal was when a teacher, student, or parent would come in and very emotionally share a concern, often demanding a quick resolution. He shared the following.

"It was apparent in their plea that they wanted me to act quickly and make a decision they would find to their liking. And I really wanted to relieve their angst! However, I sometimes failed to get both sides of a story or dig a little deeper so that I had better information and a more thorough understanding of the entire issue. I was burned more than once because I did not take the adequate time I needed to get all sides of the issue. It was embarrassing being forced to walk back a decision. In time I learned to slow down and get all the information before making a decision."

When you first assume a principalship, you will have people who will attempt to pressure you into quick decisions that serve their self-interests until they discover you are going to be deliberate and thoughtful prior to making a decision. Beware of the frantic *I need an answer now* personalities. It really pays off to analyze a situation thoroughly before seeking solutions.

Step 3: Boundary Conditions

This step relates to the specifications. What must the decision accomplish? What are the minimum goals the decision must attain? It makes sense that prior to any decisions being made the leader would have in mind some desired outcomes that would result from the decision. In short, what would be the benefits of this decision? And are there any downsides?

Step 4: What Is Right

In this step what decision meets the boundary conditions? Are the desired outcomes being met? Are there compromises that allow us to reach the minimum goals we set out to attain?

A word about compromise. There is an old expression that half a loaf of bread is better than none. When negotiating, we usually have to give up something to get something. One superintendent always felt that a good bargain was when neither side came away feeling they got everything or lost everything. In a good bargain both sides compromise!

Step 5: Building to Action (Converting the Decision)

When building an action plan, Drucker shares that there are four distinct questions to be addressed:

1. Who has to know the decision?
2. What action has to be taken?
3. Who is to implement the decision?
4. What has to be done so that people can implement the decision (tools, resources, time to move the decision to action)?

Particular emphasis should be placed on question 4. Often we proceed with a professional development plan but fail to give teachers the time and resources to roll out the plan to fruition. Or when monitoring progress or administering assessments, we do not have data warehouses and software in place to gather data and have the data inform instruction. Leaders must see that the time, tools, and resources are in place if teachers are to meet a charge or implement a change successfully.

Step 6: Feedback—Monitor and Assess Results

Once a decision is made and implemented, it next has to be monitored for progress and feedback. Decisions may go wrong in not achieving the desired outcomes. For a leader it is sometimes difficult to *let go* of an initiative that he or she was really invested in. However, if it is not rendering results, the leader must have the courage to abandon the plan or make changes to it. Consistent and timely monitoring is important because it may lead to certain modifications or tweaks that keep the desired outcomes in play.

THE HOTTER FOUR-FACTOR ANALYSIS

While the Drucker model offers a solid management base for considering decisions, another model for decision making was shared by Professor Suzanne Hotter at the University of Wisconsin in 1998 with her graduate students. It is called the Hotter Four-Factor Analysis.

The basic premise of the Hotter Four-Factor Analysis is that in any decision at least one of the following four dimensions is prevalent. And at times there may be two, three, or maybe all four dimensions interwoven in a decision. The four dimensions are the following:

- *Ethical dimension:* Can I look in the mirror after making this decision? Is it right per the values I live by? Did I attempt to be fair and truthful?

- *Political dimension:* What is the impact in terms of gaining majority support, influence, and backing? What do I have to do to win on this initiative or issue? What leverage do I need to have?
- *Legal dimension:* Can I do this without breaking the law, policy, or the tradition or unwritten rules and guidelines of an organization, family, or government body?
- *Financial dimension:* Can I afford this? Are the resources adequate?

Again all decisions have at least one of these dimensions, and some may have multiple or all four! When there is more than one factor, we have to decide which dimension carries the most weight. The matrix shown in table 9.1 serves as a good visual in utilizing this model.

Table 9.1.   Hotter: The Four-Factor Analysis

	Ethical	Legal	Financial	Political
Who				
What				
Why				
When				
Where				

Leaders are often faced with making some unpopular decisions. The Drucker and Hotter decision-making models can prevent hasty, poorly thought out decisions. It would seem apparent that decisions would be easier if in fact there is a policy in place because it should always be followed. However, not all decisions are black and white, in fact there is often a lot of gray.

Here is a case study that a professor describe as a "dirty dilemma." Read this case study carefully and then imagine yourself as the principal. How would you address this matter?

A DIRTY DILEMMA: KEITH THE HIGH JUMPER

It is Wednesday, May 25. Keith Eagle just made history the previous Saturday when he high jumped 6'10" in the district track meet. He not only established a new school record but a prep state record in Wisconsin as well. According to his coach, he has cleared 7' in practice and all track enthusiasts have their eyes on him as they anticipate Keith clearing 7' at the state meet on Saturday.

Keith is a nice young man, well mannered, and he is very well liked by his peers, teachers, and coaches. He is fun-loving guy. He struggles to get Cs but he knows better than to bring home a D or F on his report card. He comes from an African American family with three siblings, raised by their mother. Mrs. Eagle is a hard-working lady who is employed by the school system as a custodian in one of the district's elementary schools. Keith took the ACT exam three times. His best score was a 13. Despite his athletic prowess, Keith could not get admitted into a university or college.

Keith, with the support of his mother and grandma (also a strong influence), enlisted in the navy. He is to report to the naval training center in San Diego at the end of July. But before doing this, Keith had some unfinished business—winning the state high jump competition and clearing 7'. Interest grows as Keith is featured in the Prep Sport Section of USA Today. He is putting his hometown on the map!

On the hot afternoon of Wednesday, May 25, Keith and a couple of his friends decide that rather than go to study hall sixth hour, they should head across the river to the Dairy Queen and have some ice cream. Keith did not think this would be any big deal; besides, he would be back in plenty of time for seventh hour government class. So he leaves with his buddies for the Dairy Queen.

The following morning, Thursday, the athletic director (AD) is informed by the attendance office that Keith was truant from study hall. The athletic code clearly states that if a student athlete is truant from a class or classes for the day or any part of it, he or she is ineligible for the next competition. The AD is hoping Keith had a good excuse. He finds Keith after first hour and asks him where he was the previous day during sixth hour when he had study hall. Keith is straightforward and tells about the trip to Dairy Queen, having no idea of the seriousness of the consequences that might result.

When the new athletic code was put in, consistency in enforcement was stressed. The previous code was perceived as unfair because of claims of favoritism. There was also a thought that the school needed to "crack down" and get tougher on athletes who were not perceived as good "characters." The AD had worked hard to enforce the new code and now this! The track coach is distraught when he hears the news that Keith will likely be ineligible for the state meet. At this point only the AD, the coach, the study hall aide, and the attendance clerk know about this situation.

The AD takes the issue to the principal. It is 11:00 a.m. on Thursday. The AD and the track coach know that like all athletic code offenses that are controversial, the principal must be kept informed. Both hope he might have an idea. The state high jump prelims begin on Friday, just about twenty-four hours away!

1. Using the Hotter four-factor analysis tool, which of the components seem to come into play the most?

    a. Ethical

      b. Political
      c. Financial
      d. Legal

  2. If you are the principal what do you do?

- Make a decision on the matter
- Refer to the superintendent
- Tell the AD it is his responsibility to handle it

The educational leadership classes are invariably split on whether Keith should be ineligible or allowed to compete in the state meet. Handbooks typically approved by School Boards are an extension of School Board policy, so why is this case not cut and dry for those who side on suspending Keith? Per the Hotter Four-Factor Analysis, all four dimensions seem to be in play. Which dimension should carry the most weight? Let's examine this a little more closely.

Ethically, can the principal live with him- or herself by not allowing Keith to jump? Or is the principal ethically wrong to not follow the code of conduct and allow Keith to jump?

Politically, are there ramifications for the school and community if Keith does not jump? Will the African American community rise up sensing that if Keith were white, the principal would look the other way? And if in fact Keith were white and from a more affluent family would his family seek legal relief and an injunction allowing Keith to jump? Or if Keith is allowed to jump are there not claims again of favoritism that will surface per the inconsistent administration of the code of conduct?

Legally, this case certainly has some considerations, as noted earlier. How many instances have occurred in which school discipline decisions have been litigated in court? Would Keith's family have a case if he is denied the opportunity to compete? Could the principal, AD, or coach possibly have their jobs in jeopardy or be disciplined for not enforcing the code?

Financially, and closely related to the political and legal dimensions, unforeseen legal costs might result from any decision made per the disposition of this case.

The purpose behind using this case study is to illustrate that not all decisions are cut and dry. In fact, there is often a lot of gray that is gut wrenching! The disposition of this case could be decided either way with good arguments to support either position: suspension or allowing Keith to jump.

The principal in this case allowed Keith to jump. Why? He found a loophole in the fifth paragraph of the code with this sentence: "The athletic code clearly states that if a student athlete is truant from a class or classes for the day or any part of it, he or she is ineligible for the next competition."

Keith was not truant from a class; he was truant from a *study hall.* In an honest disclosure, when the code was written, the intent really was directed at skipping any part of the school day. However, in this sentence it says *class*!

Prior to making a final decision, the principal called the AD down and asked him to review all athletic suspensions since the implementation of the code. A half hour later he returned and informed the principal that in all previous athletic suspensions, student athletes had missed a class. In short there was not a case of a student athlete being suspended solely due to missing a study hall. In all other cases, if students missed a study hall, they also missed a class. This was the out!

The principal did call Keith in. With the full support of his mother and grandmother, an alternative punishment was assigned to Keith: helping the maintenance department with a trenching task the following Monday following the state meet, on the first day of summer vacation.

The principal did not inform the superintendent of the incident. Conventional wisdom would indicate he should have. Everyone included in this case study, the AD, coach, and attendance clerk, were relieved to learn of the decision. Had the principal informed the superintendent, would he have been overruled? Would the superintendent have called all seven Board members, possibly getting divergent views on the disposition of this case? Admittedly the principal noted, "I took a gamble, and sometimes you have decisions where you just make a call, and I wanted to be the one to make it."

In looking at the four dimensions of this case, the principal felt the *ethical* piece of this decision trumped all other considerations. He did not feel he could look in the mirror and shave if this young man was denied the greatest opportunity he may ever have in his life: to be a state champion and a national prep track and field record holder! Keith went on to win the state championship, but he did not clear seven feet. Six weeks later he was in San Diego, beginning his naval training.

As noted earlier, a decision either way could be defended. The professor noted, "It did not matter to me which way students came down per a decision on Keith. I was more interested in the thought process of arriving at the decision."

INVESTIGATIONS

When investigations are necessary, one thing to keep in mind is to not rush. Take your time getting the facts and all sides of the issue. A young dean of students learned a lesson the hard way in relaying the following story.

"I was convinced that a student named Scott had stolen a practice football jersey from another player, Jim. Scott was a freshman who had been in

my office for several handbook infractions but nothing ever too serious. In interviewing Jim, he convinced me that Scott was wearing his jersey and he could even identify some marks on the old jersey. I brought both boys into my office and the accusation ensued. Jim was vehement that Scott was wearing his jersey, and Scott was equally defiant that the jersey was passed down from his brother. I was in a hurry to get this issue resolved and I did not believe Scott. I informed him that I expected him to bring that jersey in to me the next day clean and folded and that if he continued to lie, he would be in more trouble!

"Well, about three hours later that afternoon, Jim's mother called and informed me that she found Jim's jersey in the wash! Boy did I have egg on my face. I called Scott in and I sincerely apologized for not believing him. He reluctantly accepted my apology, but he left my office still feeling upset about the experience. It took me quite a while to build back the rapport I once had with Scott, and I doubt he ever respected me as much as he had before this incident."

While this experience was not as serious as many other investigations, it bears out the danger of rushing to judgment. When conducting investigations, take the adequate time necessary to complete your work thoroughly.

REVISITING DECISIONS

Always reserve the right to reflect and revisit previous decisions. A guiding proviso in rendering decisions publicly is to state up front that based on the best information we have at this time, we have arrived at this decision.

Information and circumstances can change over time, and when they do you may choose to change a decision or policy. A good example is the use of cell phones in school. I recall banning them in the early 2000s. Then, as technology advanced and Bring Your Own Device initiatives became popular, policies changed in becoming more permissive.

Some may accuse you of waffling or flip-flopping when you reverse or modify decisions, but as information changes, the prudent action may be to change or revise a previous decision in moving an organization or school forward.

In closing out this chapter, a common theme related to decision making seems to indicate that the best decisions are not made in haste. Moreover, being deliberate in seeking all the information needed to make a prudent decision will serve a leader well. In addition, we learned in this chapter that not all decisions are cut and dry, and some decisions need to be revisited as new and better information becomes available to us.

SUMMARY QUESTIONS TO PONDER

- Should all decisions be made based solely on policy?
- Upon reflection, are there decisions you wish you could have back?
- Do you feel comfortable changing a decision or reversing yourself when more information becomes available over time? Or are you afraid of being accused of waffling?
- What has been the toughest decision you have had to make in your present role?

Part III

The Superintendency, Board of Education, and Life Balance

Chapter Ten

The Superintendency

You Cannot Do It Alone

It is often stated that the most important decision a Board of Education (Board) will make is the appointment of a superintendent. Who will Board members duly elected by the citizens of a community entrust to carry out district policy and oversee the day to day operations of the school district?

A superintendent search is a daunting process. Most Boards will seek the help of a consultant, a consulting firm, or their state Board organization that specializes in such services. Many of the national firms have a wide net from which to recruit candidates. The cost of hiring search consultants and firms can be considerable. However, it will be viewed as a good investment if the candidate chosen proves to be an excellent leader.

Typically, the consultant will do most of the upfront work and screening and bring to the Board a slate of finalists that usually ranges from three to five candidates. In most communities the selection of the district leader is of high interest, and the local press is very motivated to learn the names of finalists. Once finalists are selected, their names and where they have practiced become public record. Candidates have to be prepared for this as the news reaches their home district.

Superintendents who are actively searching for new positions are wise to inform their current Board of their intentions. Invariably they will need some solid references in seeking new employment, so it makes sense to be honest and upfront. If you are seeking your first superintendency, be prepared for the public scrutiny that may come with your candidacy.

THROWING YOUR HAT IN THE RING: PREPARATIONS
PRIOR TO APPLYING FOR A SUPERINTENDENCY

There are several steps a candidate should prepare for prior to seeking a superintendency. Here are some tips:

1. Make sure your certifications and licensing are up to date and will meet the job specifications of the role you are seeking. Great opportunities can come up rather quickly and you want to be able to present your full application and papers in a timely fashion. You must be fully certified prior to the stated starting date of the new job. Pending certifiable candidates who may be finishing up an endorsement or degree should indicate the anticipated date of certification and degree conferral.

2. Update your résumé on a regular basis, maybe yearly or even more frequently if you anticipate a career move. Your résumé should give insight into your rich experiences that make you a viable candidate. Include up-to-date references with complete contact information (phone numbers and email addresses).

3. Be prepared to apply electronically using the templates most search firms and districts now rely on for applications and the information they desire. It might be helpful to have a trusted friend with tech savvy help you in this process if you are fearful of making errors.

4. Before applying to a district, do your homework and research. Study Board minutes for the previous two years, look at their Strategic Plan, and find out what the key issues are. Visit the community, and, if you know citizens and educators in the community, talk to them. In short, you want to find out if you would be a "good fit" for the job. The mistake many candidates make is being overly enamored with the salary and benefits a district might offer. While this is important, most experienced superintendents would rate this far secondary compared with working with a trusting and competent Board.

5. Some key references you would want to secure well in advance: If it is your first superintendency, you want references from your current superintendent and past superintendents, supervisors, and Board members who know of your work. Solid teacher references are also important that might speak to your instructional and management skills along with your character and sense of fairness. It would also be helpful to include parents, community members, and students (especially if you were a high school principal) who could validate your fine work in the past. Another reference experienced and new superintendents should not overlook is a reference from the teacher union president, if possible. Be assured that the district teacher association

where you are applying will want to do a scouting report on all finalists who might eventually become their superintendent.

THE INTERVIEW

It is an exciting time when you get that call and invitation to interview. By the time you receive the call, hopefully you will have done your homework and determined that this indeed is a district that looks like a good fit. Hopefully your spouse or significant other and family are on board with you. It will be an adjustment for them, especially children, to leave their friends and schools in relocating to a new community. For your spouse or significant other, it may mean leaving a job he or she has enjoyed in making the transition for the sake of your career advancement.

Listed here are some thoughts regarding preparation for the interview and what to expect:

1. Consider what you will wear to the interview well in advance. Find something you really like and feel comfortable in. Maybe a spouse or trusted friend will help you with your choice.
2. Allow plenty of time to get to the interview site. You don't want to come in huffing and puffing. You want to enter the interview room relaxed. Find the location an hour ahead of time. Then drive to the nearest Starbucks or coffee shop where you can relax a bit, go over some notes you have prepared, and take a last look in a mirror.
3. Arrive fifteen minutes ahead of time, check in with the receptionist, and breathe easy!
4. Be prepared to meet with multiple people in the initial interview. When you walk in, take your cues from the chair of the interview. If there is an opportunity to greet and shake hands, that is a good first gesture.
5. Listen closely to the instructions about how the interview will be conducted, especially if the chair indicates a time limit for questions in keeping your answers brief and concise. Don't be afraid to pause and reflect before answering a question. That tiny bit of time for reflection will allow you to answer the question thoughtfully rather than impulsively.
6. Answer all questions honestly per your beliefs. By doing this you will stay consistent and your overall interview performance will leave a solid impression. This is far preferable to candidates who provide responses they believe the interviewing audience wants to hear.
7. Have questions prepared. Typically, you will have an opportunity to ask a couple of questions at the end of the interview. You don't want

to wear out your welcome with a long list of questions, but a couple of well-thought-out key questions will be received well and will show the interest and preparation you have done.

8. Most finalists will go through a grueling second interview. Prior to the day of the interview, be well rested. You will need to have a lot of stamina. The day may start as early as 8:00 a.m. and not end until late that evening. The day may include separate meetings with teacher representatives including union leadership, principals, and administrators, visits to district schools, meetings with community members, business people, Chamber of Commerce directors, parents, and Board members. Be prepared that these meetings may be very public. You may be asked to give a presentation in a public forum where all stakeholders, citizens, and the local press are invited and allowed to ask questions. Oftentimes at the end of an interview day you may be invited by the Board for a dinner meeting. In all sessions you will want to remain alert and be a great listener, carefully and honestly answering questions and inquiries.

9. If you have a dinner with the Board, keep in mind while they are interviewing you that you are seeking to learn about them and how they interact and view the role of the superintendent. One superintendent made the following observation.

"The interview day went really well. It was only at the dinner with the Board that I began to have some concerns. My wife who was with me had the same vibes. It was apparent that this Board was far different from the Board I currently served that was respectful of my role in running the day-to-day operations.

"Before the meal was finished it became clear that these Board members were very accustomed to micromanaging, and the retiring previous superintendent had allowed them to do so. As the conversations went on, both the Board and I could see that we were far apart on roles and relationships as it related to the Board and the superintendent. I still hoped I would get the appointment thinking I could change some of their thinking.

"My wife, ever the honest voice in my life, cautioned me on the ride home by asking, 'Do you want to be directed by them to make decisions that you now have the freedom to make on your own now?' She added, 'I doubt they will prefer you over the other finalist because you stood up to them in clearly delineating how you viewed the role of the Board and the superintendent, and I was proud you did!' I swallowed hard!

"She was right. Two days later I received a call that the other finalist was chosen. Looking back, I was fortunate not to get that job. It was a miserable run for the superintendent who was selected, mired

in micromanaging and controversial issues. Instead I enjoyed ten more years in my current role with supportive Board members who let me do my job."

YOU GET THE JOB OFFER, THEN WHAT?

After being vetted thoroughly and interviewing, there is great elation when you receive the call that you are being offered the superintendent appointment. However, there is one more very important step, and that is negotiating your first contract. Typically, by this point in the process, a Board does not want to risk losing their first choice, but you may need to negotiate salary, vacation time, and some other perks that you believe are commensurate with the job before accepting. This is the time to iron out such matters. It is important to take some time to go over your contract and be sure it meets with your satisfaction.

A hiring Board will usually be pretty accommodating as long as contract requests are reasonable. These matters sometimes take a couple of days. Most state superintendent agencies offer a service in which they will review a contract in advising a member or soon to be member. Another option would be to have a lawyer who is familiar with school law and administrative contracts to review your new contract. It's worth the fee you will be charged to have this legal review.

A second but very important piece of advice is not to submit a letter of resignation to your present district Board until you know that your hiring has been approved by the Board of your new district. Last-minute issues sometimes occur, so never leave a job until you know for certain you have a job in another district. Some superintendents have learned the hard way, finding themselves completely out of a job when their resignations are not rescinded after the new job falls through.

THE FIRST HUNDRED DAYS

Building your knowledge base in your new district takes time. You often hear the premise that when a new president is elected in the United States, the first one hundred days are critical in setting the agenda and carrying out campaign promises for the first four-year term.

Well, the first hundred days are critical in the superintendency as well, not so much for setting an agenda as it is for building relationships and trust. Getting to know your Board, administrative team (central office and principals), schools, teachers, parents, business people, community leaders, and students and giving them a chance to know you are the most important first steps in the first one hundred days.

Of the communicative skills you will need to employ, listening is the most important. Sure, you will be asked to make presentations and speeches in meeting groups for the first time, but nothing in that first one hundred days is more important than *listening*. As the saying sometimes goes, "we learn more from listening than speaking."

Once your feet are on the ground and the one hundred days have passed, you can then begin to put your influence into an academic, fiscal, and communication agenda. You will now be better for it because you were respectful and diligent in building relationships first.

Of course there are some pressing issues and dilemmas you will inherit, and they will need your immediate attention. For these you will have to intensify your listening sessions. This will give you confidence to make decisions and recommendations to the Board.

One of the things that will surprise you, if you are moving from the principal ranks to the superintendency, is that for most decisions you will have more time to make them. As a principal you often had to make quick decisions that had better be right. As superintendent, while the stakes for decisions may be immense, you have more time for reflection, consultation, and ultimately deciding a course of action.

ARE SUPERINTENDENTS AGENTS OF THE BOARD OR THEIR CONSCIENCE?

Superintendents often find themselves in a conundrum. Are they agents of the Board or are they the leader of the educational team? Needless to say, they have to figure out the balance. Successful superintendents will follow their conscience in making every effort to do what is morally and ethically sound. The key consideration is never losing sight of what will serve students best with the district mission.

There are several pathways to the superintendency. Most superintendents began their careers as teachers. However, in urban districts it's not uncommon for mayors to appoint noneducators to lead the district. In Chicago, a former city budget director served as superintendent. In fact, he went on to serve in two other urban districts, usually moving on when the politics dictated his departure.

It has become apparent that the more influence and political skill a leader can demonstrate in working with factions the more likely he or she will succeed. Being renewed for a second contract often depends on a superintendent's political savvy.

Following a teaching experience, most pathways to the superintendency either go through the principal ranks directly to the superintendency or from the principalship to a central office role in either instruction, pupil services, or the business side of the district. Whatever the pathway, once in the superintendent chair, no other experience has fully prepared you for what you are about to embark on. However, this is not to be feared but embraced. There is honor and prestige in being selected to lead a school district. You are viewed as one of the major leaders in the community.

THE IMPORTANCE OF DISTRIBUTIVE LEADERSHIP

One certainty about the superintendency is that you cannot do the job alone! You will need the help of others. In a distributive leadership model, the superintendent must be a great judge of talent in the appointments of central office directors and principals who will in turn hire great faculty and staff.

A good superintendent will allow his or her leadership team to do their jobs, resisting the temptation to micromanage. On establishing job descriptions and expectations with benchmarks to review progress, there is a mutual trust and belief in the team members.

One superintendent likened his leadership flowchart to an NFL head coach. Jerry Glanville, a former NFL coach with the Houston Oilers and Atlanta Falcons, once coined the phrase, "N-F-L stands for not for long." NFL coaches are expected to lead their teams to playoff appearances and championships. Superintendents are expected to produce favorable student achievement results in their capacity to lead a school district.

Figure 10.1 shows a metaphorical analogy one superintendent patterned after the NFL. He established this flow chart to illustrate his systems approach in his school district.

This metaphorical analogy may seem simplistic but does convey that the superintendent as the head coach needs outstanding coordinators and coaches in all phases of the school district's operations.

The academic agenda is the educational plan that has been strategically coordinated to meet desired outcomes. Like football, this is your offense, and you want to score! For this to happen you need strong leadership from your director of instruction (or chief academic officer [CAO]). The director of instruction or CAO has several offensive coaches in the central office as shown in the figure. Principals (position coaches) carry out the offensive game plan in the buildings.

Too often a district will inhibit itself when it begins strategic planning. The academic agenda is severely compromised by conservative fiscal thinking. A prevalent notion that we cannot afford or sustain certain programs and services or our property taxes will be too high can often dominate some creative possibility planning. This shortchanges our youth. Of course fiscal constraints are a reality, but they should never be a *starting point* that stifles planning that could advance the access and opportunities for students.

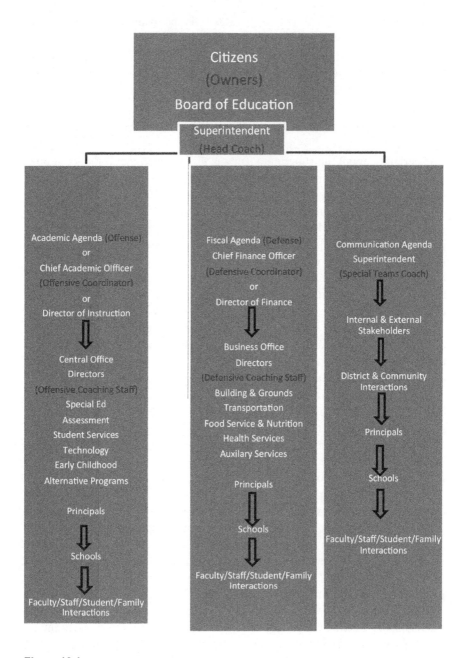

Figure 10.1.

Build the academic agenda first and then worry about financing it. Sure there will always be some tough financial decisions, but they should not come until after an academic agenda has been constructed and programs and opportunities for students can be reviewed.

The fiscal agenda is your defense. The business side of the district has to be fastidious in forecasting and committed to finding every conceivable dollar to support the academic agenda (offense) and help it score.

Some directors of finance (chief financial officers [CFOs]) are too detached from the academic agenda. They worry more about the ledger sheet and building their fund balances, which while necessary, are not the most important priority. A superintendent cannot let CFOs be naysayers or final decision makers impacting programmatic opportunities. A superintendent should press the CFO and the business office staff to find savings and revenue streams.

A CFO (director of business) is a well-trained professional who has specific knowledge and skills with school finance formulas, taxation, state aid, insurance, and debt service. He or she is your defensive coordinator. The CFO also has many defensive coaches. They provide great leadership for auxiliary services. The greatest service the CFO provides the superintendent is to offer options regarding available fiscal resources. Too many superintendents literally yield the decisions to the CFO who impacts the academic programming. That can't happen.

What an outstanding superintendent will do is make sure that the CAO and the CFO work well together. These are high-level positions, and the superintendent has to press both of them to bring forward a strong academic agenda that is supported by the fiscal agenda.

On establishing a strong academic agenda, supported by the fiscal agenda, the next most important piece is establishing the communication agenda. As superintendent, you are the face of the district. In the metaphoric NFL analogy, this is the special teams.

The special teams phase of the team, like in the NFL, is very important and helps you win! A superintendent must engage all stakeholders, keeping them informed and most importantly listening to concerns, ideas, and needs. The messaging from the superintendent to internal and external stakeholders is so important. In larger districts, a public relations director or spokesperson is often charged with communication and messaging.

The district must convey genuine caring and investment in both sending out information and receiving feedback. The connection the superintendent has with the entire learning community and citizens has to be positive. Relationship building is critical, and superintendents who do not take this seriously do not last long. Nobody is more responsible for the communication agenda than the superintendent.

You will notice the principal appears on all three agendas: the academic, fiscal, and communication agendas. This again, as noted earlier in the book, emphasizes just how important the leadership of a principal is in helping a building and a district flourish.

The main role of the principal as a position coach is to hire great people. A principal more than any other leader must be able to build capacity in his or her staff. Professional development (PD) is a key component in an academic agenda. This often is led by the office of instruction and CAO. However, it is the principal who plays the biggest role in making sure the PD takes hold in a building. Thus it is the superintendent who must select outstanding principals and maintain a close working relationship with them.

While the superintendent is the face of the district, the principal is the face of his or her learning community. That superintendent-principal relationship has to be healthy and built on trust. A superintendent who does not pay enough attention to principals or overdelegates mostly to the CAO misses an opportunity to have a closer bond at the school level. Of course in large urban districts it would be impossible for a superintendent to work directly with principals without a lot of help from CAOs and offices of instruction. However, the great majority of school districts have fewer than ten thousand pupils. This allows the superintendent to work closely with principals.

In the metaphorical schematic, the principal also appears on the fiscal agenda (defense). As the instructional leader and manager of the building, the principal will have considerable influence on where funds are allocated in building budgets.

MEETINGS WITH CENTRAL OFFICE
ADMINISTRATORS AND PRINCIPALS

That old saying that "you can't live with or live without meetings" certainly holds some truth for a superintendent. Keeping tabs on everything that goes on in a school district takes constant communication. The following model for meetings worked with one superintendent who felt it kept him in the loop.

"I would have a short meeting with my director of instruction, special education director, and finance director every morning for a quick ten- to fifteen-minute briefing on pressing issues in the district and daily calendar events we needed to prepare ourselves for. It was a quick in and out to get a pulse on the day. We all benefited from listening to each other and what we all had on the docket.

"On Tuesdays we would have an extended cabinet meeting that in addition to the directors of instruction, finance, and special education would also include the directors of technology, building and maintenance, and at times the director of food and nutrition. It was at this meeting we would take the

calendar out a month to two months, review the most pressing issues each director was working on, and prepare for the monthly Board of Education meeting. We would also review agenda items for the full administrative team.

"*We also took time in these meetings to evaluate and discuss how events, plans, and goals were progressing. It would usually take two hours or a good part of the morning depending on the depth of the items we had to cover. Minutes were always kept to make sure we followed up on matters.*

"*For full administrative monthly administrative meetings, held on the second Tuesday of each month, all principals, assistant principals, and directors would be present. The meetings usually ran from 2:00 to 4:00 p.m. Sometimes we had to go longer but rarely later than 5:00 p.m. Prior to the meeting agenda being sent out, I would ask for agenda items leaders might want to include for the meeting.*

"*We always began with a professional learning community activity that each administrator took a turn leading. This kept us aligned with our distributive leadership model of sharing with each other in concert with the Michael Fullan model of being lead learners! We often did a book study or addressed a currently trending topic in education. From there we went on to district and building topics and business. These always included some monitoring of strategic plan goals for the year and reports from the lead administrator for each goal in reviewing progress. Again, we would have an assistant take minutes so follow through of actions and decisions would not slip through the cracks.*

"*As a superintendent I tried to find the 'sweet spot' in not holding too many administrative meetings yet covering what we needed to cover. I also felt it was important to enhance the professional growth of the entire administrative team. Things did not always go so 'rosy.' At times we had some pretty spirited conversations that once in a while crossed the line of decorum. When this began to happen we would always direct ourselves back to our mission. This kept us focused on purposeful engagement, team work, and consensus in moving the district forward as a leadership team.*

"*There were some occasions when we needed to call an emergency administrative meeting for a single agenda issue. These took place only when necessary. Respecting the time of your team members amid their immense responsibilities should be a strong consideration when deciding to hold meetings.*"

Always seeking balance and effectiveness in the use of time and resources, a superintendent must deploy strategies that bring out the best in his or her leadership team.

WORKING WITH UNIONS AND BARGAINS

We always have to remember that we are in a very intense human business. For us to be successful, we need to build cultures that are ingratiating to all who fall under our leadership. In the United States, a current worry we have is that fewer candidates are entering our schools of education in our universities and colleges. Hopefully this trend will reverse itself in the future.

Since the early 2000s, many school districts have struggled to hire highly qualified teachers and staff by the start of each school year. While this formerly was a problem for urban districts, it has now become a great concern for small rural districts, midsize towns, and even some suburban districts, especially in disciplines like special education, math, science, and English language learning.

It's not surprising that union/Board/administrative relations often become strained. Working conditions are very important to teachers and staff. They want to work in a place where they are fairly compensated, the working conditions are safe, and the resources are adequate for them to do their jobs.

In many states, governors and legislators have stifled teacher compensation in efforts to balance state budgets and hold the line on local property taxes. Thus the collateral damage is now being realized per inequities across districts when comparing per pupil spending. Young people are leaving the profession before the age of thirty, and great teachers are retiring earlier.

The accountability movement and reliance on standardized tests as a measure of teacher effectiveness have resulted in many teachers feeling overwhelmed and stressed. Superintendents and principals have to intercede and support teachers in reducing some roles and responsibilities that aren't impactful for student achievement.

In working with teacher unions, it is good to meet regularly with the union leadership. A breakfast or early dinner is a great way to meet monthly and converse with union presidents and leaders to share mutual concerns and differing positions on issues. These bread-breaking meetings help build rapport. This underpinning right from the start of a new superintendency can reap many benefits down the road.

Bargaining is usually arduous. Invariably settlements usually come down to money and working conditions. Tensions at various bargaining sessions can run high. What is important for a superintendent is to never allow the relationship with union leaders to become so strained that it is severed. The superintendent should make every effort to instill this same spirit with his or her Board.

In bargaining, attorneys and lawyers for both the teacher's union and the Board often become involved. This is often necessary when final details, impasses, and mediations are part of the bargain. However, the relationship between the superintendent and union leadership even in bargaining has to remain respectful with the superintendent taking most of the responsibility for this.

Just as the superintendent has to answer to a board, a union president has to answer to his or her membership if ratification of a contract is to be reached. When a superintendent is respectful of this and keeps the channels of communication open, there is more likelihood that fair concessions on both sides might be reached.

One superintendent described his role in negotiations in the following manner.

"When working with the Board and determining negotiation objectives and goals, I always wanted to make sure that I pushed the Board as far as I could in compensating our teachers and staff fairly. For non-money, small impact items the union wanted, if feasible I urged the Board to accept them.

"I was often a bit disheartened that some teachers were not always appreciative or understanding of my efforts. However, I took solace in knowing that the union leaders understood. While protecting the Boards' interests, union leaders understood I pushed as hard as I could when it came to compensation and working conditions. In sharing forecasts honestly along with pay scenarios, the union leadership, while not always totally agreeing, respected my efforts to be as fair as possible."

This superintendent also met and bargained with unions for custodians (local AFSCME affiliate) and the clerical staff. For all three unions, monthly meetings usually over breakfast were held to keep the communication lines open and be proactive in heading off any grievances.

In short, neither side should walk away from a bargain feeling totally happy or angry. Compromise and meeting at a settlement point where relations remain intact are where you want to be. Again, as the old saying goes, "Half a loaf of bread is better than none, fight to live another day to get the other half."

COMMUNITY INVOLVEMENT, ADVISORY COMMITTEES, BOOSTER CLUBS, AND TASK FORCES

In an earlier chapter, some ideas were shared in terms of a questionnaire that new superintendents or principals could utilize in accelerating their knowledge base in a new district. The questionnaire would likely yield the names of city officials, council members, business and industry leaders and executives, clergy, county officials, leaders of service groups, and members of nonprofit agencies. Many will be eager to meet you.

In many towns, the school district will be one of the largest employers. The economic reach of a school district is important for the vitality of many communities. It serves many superintendents well to join a service club like

Rotary, Lions, or Kiwanis where they meet other community members and build relationships. Down the road these ties can prove very useful when seeking community support for referendums. It is also important for a super-intendent to encourage leadership team members to become active in the community. One superintendent shared the following.

"I wanted all my principals and central office leaders to wear another hat in the community. Coaching little league, scout leaders, service club mem-bers, or being active in their churches. That investment in the community pays dividends! I also encouraged them to live in the community where people would see them in the grocery stores and businesses, buying their cars locally, and pumping their gas. Citizens notice when a high-salaried leader is invested in the community and contributes to the local economy."

As for advisory committees, many superintendents have standing adviso-ry committees that meet monthly or quarterly. This group is usually made up of parents, teachers, and business people who can serve as message givers and message deliverers. The superintendent can get a strong and reliable perspective on what is happening within a school or the district. In turn, advisory members often can help spread the message the superintendent wants to circulate in the schools and community.

Most districts need additional fiscal help due to resources often being scarce. This is where booster clubs and parent-teacher associations (PTAs) or organizations (PTOs) often help a school and district immensely. Catholic schools for decades have relied on booster clubs and fundraising to stay open. Now public schools find themselves looking for outside help from willing boosters!

Playgrounds, competition fields, uniforms, and transportation costs are all things that often exceed the district funding available. Thus booster clubs for sports, music, drama, and Future Farmers of America have taken a more prominent role in raising considerable funds for co-curricular activities, and in the case of PTAs or PTOs building expensive and safe playgrounds.

These boosters give of their time and energy to really help the students enjoy a great co-curricular experience. Superintendents and principals are deeply in their debt. As budgets have gotten much tighter with revenue limits, the money raised by these groups keeps valuable programs in place.

One high school principal lamenting on how her building budgets had been frozen for five straight years shared the following in her newsletter.

"Thank God for my booster clubs. Seventy-five percent of the student body is involved in some sport, music, or club. While our academics stretch and challenge the mind, it is our co-curricular programming that teach our kids how to work with others! Given the budget cuts we have endured in recent years, there is no way we could continue our co-curricular offerings if our booster clubs had not come to the rescue."

As helpful as booster clubs can be, a superintendent will need to make sure through his or her distributive leadership model to work with principals and activities and athletic directors in monitoring the fundraising and spending of these organizations. The director of finance familiar with annual audit practices should be very involved in the oversight of booster club funds in preventing any sort of malfeasance.

One Catholic priest who was principal of a north central Iowa Catholic high school was once asked by a teacher working on his principal license how he worked with booster clubs. His quick response was, "I keep them broke!" What is clear in the priest's answer is whoever controls the money also controls the power and influence.

There have been many cases especially in recent years where booster clubs have raised well into six figures in their fundraising. At times powerful boosters have used this leverage in attempts to sway and talk administrations into decisions that are not aligned with the mission or values of the district. Just as abuses have occurred at the collegiate level, they have also become more prevalent in affluent high schools and school districts. Embezzlement cases and unchecked fiscal control can cause a lot of grief and embarrassment for a superintendent.

A good practice with any booster club is to make sure its bylaws are legally reviewed by a school attorney and clearly under the jurisdiction of the school board per school board policy. The director of finance or CFO should give all booster club budgets a thorough review. They are trained to discover improprieties that a principal or activities director might accidentally miss.

A good check and balance would be to make sure an individual booster club officer cannot sign off on expenditures alone. Multiple booster club officer signatures should be required.

Booster clubs should present an annual budget in the early fall to the superintendent and Board. The annual booster budget plan should indicate a budget balance, fundraising plans, projects to fund in the given year, and a plan that clearly shows how the revenues will be spent down. At the end of the year the balance should be modest (unless for example there was a multiyear project like purchasing bleachers, where a carryover might be deemed appropriate). The superintendent and Board should receive an end of the year budget report. The director of finance should give this close examination in making sure it is compliant with accounting practices and will pass muster in an audit.

Task forces and ad-hoc committees are often formed when a superintendent and a Board recognize that citizen involvement and leadership is the best avenue to a desired outcome. This is very prevalent when a school district needs to pass a referendum for building a new school or making decisions that are sure to provoke great community interest.

Some School Board members resent the formation of task forces, feeling they, not appointed citizens, should mull over recommendations and be final decision makers on major initiatives. However, most School Board members see the wisdom in expanding the perspective by appointing a task force in studying a big-impact issue and making recommendations to a board. Appointing a task force is a School Board function!

A mistake that can be made in forming a task force is in selecting only pro–school district advocates. There needs to be a balance that would include others, even those known to be critical of past district decisions. An effort should be made to include parents, seniors, people of color, and ethnicities from various socioeconomic backgrounds. The community will view the membership skeptically if there is not diverse representation with varied perspectives.

Ideally a successful task force will complete its charge from the Board and render options for consideration. The timeline for a task force to complete its work must be long enough that the members can study the issue thoroughly, while having adequate time to develop viable solutions. Typically, task forces disband within a year's time or less. A skilled facilitator, preferably not seen as partisan to any possible outcome, can make sure all perspectives are shared prior to arriving at conclusions and making recommendations to the Board.

At the completion of a task force's work, recommendations are forwarded to the Board. The Board can accept in part or in whole any of the options the task force forwards to them. A slippery slope for a Board is to reject or not accept major portions of a task force recommendation. That can lead to citizens refusing to be a part of a task force in the future. It also raises suspicion that the Board from the beginning had made up its mind and the task force was merely a façade.

Overall the use of task forces has been positive for many communities. It signals an effort on the part of the superintendent and the Board to hear out the citizenry on important decisions. Some of these decisions may result in million-dollar expenditures that include new facilities, improved opportunities for youth, and higher property taxes that underscore a community's desire to invest in finer education.

One Midwest superintendent observed the following.

"It is never the superintendent or the Board that gets a referendum passed. Moreover, it is the task force or citizenry group who can galvanize a community and get out the yes vote that determines the fate of referendum questions put forth before the electorate.

"Superintendents who think they and their administrative teams alone can pass a referendum are headed for heartache! I know, I tried it! The lesson learned was to charge a task force to come up with recommendations for the Board as it moves forward in getting referendum questions on the

ballot. Citizens are more inclined to vote yes in having their taxes increased if the request is coming from fellow citizens."

SOME CLOSING THOUGHTS ON SUPERINTENDENCY

The superintendency is a prestigious position. It is a higher calling in which a community places its trust in a leader of its most important local institution! Respect for the position and performing honorably is a commitment a superintendent must make. Placing the needs of students above all else must always be at the surface of every decision. A good superintendent will always treat everyone with respect. In pressure situations, the superintendent takes the lead in modeling poise, civility, and integrity.

As superintendent you have a great opportunity to be a difference maker in the lives of students, families, teachers, staff, and your community. The superintendents who are *all in* and truly invested in their communities are the superintendents who will succeed! They defy that N-F-L not for long tag. If you give your best and always strive to do what is best for the youth in your schools and support the people who work with them daily, you will succeed and be remembered fondly!

SUMMARY QUESTIONS TO PONDER

- Are your résumé and portfolio in order for applying for a superintendency?
- What preparations and study do you feel are necessary before applying for a superintendency in another community?
- How would you feel regarding the public scrutiny that a finalist candidate may have to endure once his or her candidacy is made public?
- How would you envision working with a leadership team in the central office?
- How would you work as a superintendent with principals for your expectations of their instructional and management skills?
- What would be your comfort level in working with unions and labor groups on collective bargaining agreements?
- How comfortable are you in delegating and distributing leadership roles and responsibilities?
- How would you work with task forces, citizen committees, and booster clubs in making sure that roles and expectations were clearly defined?

Chapter Eleven

The Superintendent and the Board of Education

Roles and Relationships

The popular series *West Wing* that ran on NBC from 1999 to 2006 aired a very moving episode in its first year. It takes place in the office of the chief of staff, Leo McGary. In soliciting loyalty and honesty from each senior members of President Josiah (Jed) Bartlett's staff, McGary challenges each person by asking them who they serve. Each cabinet director responds, "I serve at the pleasure of the president of the United States."

As superintendent, you serve at the pleasure of the Board of Education (Board). Hopefully at the time of your hire, the Board is unanimous in selecting you as their top candidate. Most Boards are made up of seven members, although some have five, nine, and in a few cases even more. Board seats can be at large or members may be elected from specific boundary areas of the district. The latter is common in bigger districts and in communities and townships that may have consolidated into one larger district. Coming into a superintendency on a four-to-three or five-to-two vote can be a risky decision with a Board election looming the following spring. Regardless, it makes great sense for a new superintendent to meet his or her new Board and treat all members equally and with respect. This is not always an easy task, especially when working with a factional Board.

As noted earlier, the average tenure of superintendents is a shade over three years. Given this is the case, most Board members who serve more than one term will likely be involved in the hiring of a superintendent. It makes sense for the new superintendent and the Board to spend some time in building shared knowledge. This is where the superintendent can gage how the

Board members work with each other along with becoming familiar with the Strategic Plan and goals the Board has previously established.

It is not unusual for a new superintendent to also have new Board members just beginning their terms. They too need a strong induction process. Board work can be complex with laws and policies that must be adhered to. State School Board Associations provide great induction programs for new Board members, along with very frequent and timely professional development programs and presentations for experienced Board members.

Laws are constantly changing, and keeping your Board up to date on recent legislation, state funding, and policy is really important. It is a missed opportunity when a superintendent does not travel and attend conferences with the Board. In the down time sharing a meal at these conferences and traveling to and from the conferences, there exists a great informal opportunity for Board members and the superintendent to grow as a team. A superintendent can never lose sight of an opportunity to educate Board members and strengthen relationships.

The key role of a Board is to establish policy and provide oversight for the school district. In that oversight a Board should assure there is accountability for student achievement. The mission, vision, and beliefs should never stray from the Board focusing on student learning and continual improvement.

Holding the superintendent accountable is an important role of the Board in insisting on high expectations. Progress and evaluation of the superintendent's performance should be reviewed semiannually in January and at the end of the academic year in June, shortly after reviewing midpoint and yearly progress made on the annual goals in the Strategic Plan.

Several years ago, William Attila, a respected consultant from a prominent Illinois-based search firm, gave an interesting presentation at an American Association of School Administrators conference. In his remarks he focused on the proper roles and relationships in a Board/superintendent shared governance approach.

Attila made it sound simple by stating the Board determines the *what* policy, desired outcomes, high expectations, monitoring student achievement data, and holding the superintendent accountable for all that falls under the *what* of shared governance. The Strategic Plan falls under the ownership of the Board. It is designed to withstand superintendent and administrative turnover, while not deterring the Board from achieving the desired outcomes in a multiyear Strategic Plan.

Once the Strategic Plan outcomes are determined and policies are approved by the Board, Attila stressed it is the superintendent and his or her team that then determine the *how*. Very bluntly Attila stated, "The Board does the *what*, and the superintendent and the educational leadership team determines the *how*. Furthermore, it is critical that each stays in his or her own yard and does not try to micromanage the other's domain."

This delineation of roles makes a lot of sense. Many dysfunctional Boards meddle in operational tasks that are clearly about the *how*, and the superintendent's role. When this happens, the entire organization is disrupted and the focus on teaching, learning, and student achievement is derailed. Likewise, some superintendents come in and think they can dictate policy. That is a huge mistake that has led to short tenures for many superintendents!

The Wisconsin Association of School Boards often held trainings on Board roles in recognizing the difference between the *what* and the *how*. In fact, one superintendent remembered a discussion at the Board table in which Board members frequently remind each other, "that is a how." This is why Board training is so important.

Board members run for Board seats for any number of reasons. Most candidates truly want to contribute positively to the school district. Others may have a single issue that has motivated them to run for the Board and seek change. Still others with political ambitions may see a role on the school Board as a stepping-stone to other political positions.

Whatever the motivation a person has for running for the Board, the candidate, shortly after filing papers, should be brought in for an initial induction. This session should be hosted by the superintendent and the Board president or a veteran Board member. Between the beginning of January when most deadlines are set for filing and a February primary or early April election, there is adequate time to host such a session. Bringing all the candidates up to date on the Strategic Plan, pressing issues, and a Board member handbook is an opportunity to bring candidates up to speed.

With the help of the Board president, the superintendent should remind the Board candidates that while they may have a specific issue that is behind their candidacy for a seat, they will be expected to deal with *all* issues.

During the induction it should be stressed that the role of the Board is to hold the superintendent and educational team accountable for student achievement and continual improvement as the policy and oversight body of the shared governance approach. The Board works as a *team* to make this happen. One superintendent recalls a wise and retired doctor who served several terms on the Board, reminding Board candidates of the following: "There is no 'I' in the word 'Board.' We may not always have a unanimous vote, but once a decision is made *we all* support the Board decision."

COMMUNICATION BETWEEN THE
SUPERINTENDENT AND THE BOARD

How much and how often should the superintendent and the Board communicate? This is an important question. The safe answer is "as needed." However, except for emergency issues, weekly updates are usually adequate. Some bullet notes sent out on Fridays keeping the Board informed giving them a heads up and a reminder of events coming up. Especially if there is something that might cause some angst in the community, most superintendents and Boards work under the premise of "no surprises."

Typically, a superintendent will work closely with a Board president in setting up Board agendas or asking for advice on some matters. However, a great effort must be made to share information with all members. If one Board member contacts the superintendent or administrative team with an inquiry, then the response should be shared with *all* Board members. Failing to keep all Board members in the loop results in unhealthy Board alliances. It is important that the superintendent treats all Board members with equal respect especially in communicating.

Board Meetings

Usually a Board will meet no more than twice a month to handle the regular business of the district. A meeting cannot commence without a quorum (a majority of the Board: as an example, on a seven-person Board at least four must be present to constitute a quorum). The first meeting may be an informational meeting with committee reports. The second meeting of the month is the business meeting where action items are considered.

The Board president assigns fellow Board members to committees, like policy, finance, facilities, instruction, and so on. This distribution of duties works well as long as the whole Board ultimately receives all the information. Sometimes all of the information does not filter back to all of the Board members from a specific committee, and this is where the superintendent has to be vigilant. Thus the Board briefings described in the next heading are a way to make sure all information is shared with all Board members.

Many districts like just one regular meeting of the Board each month. This works well if all the business of the district can be addressed within two and a half hours. As one superintendent shared, "The old saying that nothing good happens after midnight applies to Board meetings as well."

Special meetings are at times necessary but should be kept to a minimum. School district citizens should feel comfortable knowing when the Board meets with regular meetings that are noticed and occur on the same corresponding days and weeks of each month (like the second and fourth Thursday).

A serious single issue can arise for which the Board may need to meet. Examples could be a serious event like a roof collapsing or a boundary change that has created community unrest.

Closed session meetings are only permissible if they meet certain state statutes. A Board can move into closed session when discussing or negotiating the purchase of property, personnel matters, or during collective bargaining negotiations. The statute for which a Board wishes to meet in closed session must be cited in the resolution to move into closed session.

In a closed session, a Board president and a superintendent have to make sure that the only discussions that take place are aligned with the resolution to move into closed session. Minutes must be kept. This is where many Boards and superintendents can get into trouble by violating the open meetings laws. If Board member conversations stray from the intended reason for going into closed session, a Board and district may find themselves in litigation.

Board Briefings

A good way to keep Board members in the loop and working with each other begins with the monthly Board meeting and building the agenda. Prior to adjourning a Board meeting, a good last agenda item is for the Board president to ask fellow Board members if there are any future agenda items the Board would like addressed. When there is consensus by Board members to have items they would like on the next or on future agendas, some planning and teamwork begins.

As noted earlier, the superintendent usually meets with the Board president to draft the next Board agenda. Sometimes the packets of information that are sent to Board members in advance of a meeting are very lengthy. It is almost unreasonable to expect the Board members to read and understand everything in the packet, especially some of the financial information.

A superintendent who worked with a five-member Board held regular briefing meetings prior to the regular meeting of the Board on the third Thursday of each month. The Friday before he would meet with the Board president and another member in a lunch or afternoon meeting and go over the entire agenda and Board packet. The following Monday, he would do the same in a breakfast meeting with two other members, and then later that Monday at a lunch meeting, or the following Tuesday morning over breakfast, he would meet with the remaining Board member. This superintendent was deliberate in making sure that the Board members rotated and had a different member with each monthly briefing. This way they got to know each other better and it prevented Board alliances that could be unhealthy.

Were the breakfast and lunch meetings necessary? Maybe not, but in most cases, food helps in creating a comfortable setting. The most important outcome of these briefings is that all Board members were prepared for the Board meeting and the options and actions they might have to consider. However, a great sidebar outcome was that the Board members got to know each other better and gained respect for the perspectives each brought to the Board.

Another advantage of the briefings was it gave the superintendent an opportunity to hear the concerns or questions the Board might have in advance of the Board meeting on that Thursday night, along with other concerns they might share unrelated to the upcoming meeting.

By Tuesday at 9:00 a.m., the superintendent could then meet with his or her cabinet and go through the agenda or concerns Board members brought up in the briefings. This allowed the superintendent to seek answers and clarifications Board members were seeking in the briefing. When Board members raised the questions at the Board table, the administrative team was ready and prepared to give thoughtful and accurate responses.

There will be questions that come up at times when a superintendent or other administrative presenters do not know the answers. The best response is to acknowledge you do not know the answer but will look into it and get back to the Board as soon as reasonable. Some superintendents and presenters will try to "wing it" only to discover later that they passed on some misinformation. This can erode Board trust, so being honest is the best response.

Briefings also dissuade some Board members who may have a penchant for "got ya" questions. They are less inclined to ask these types of questions in public, knowing their fellow Board members are aware they could have brought them up in briefings. The rest of the Board will not want to see presenters and the superintendent embarrassed in public. The briefings are a cornerstone in the trust and relationships the superintendent has built with the Board.

A meeting of the Board is a meeting of the Board members that is held in the public. With the exception of an agenda item that asks for public comment, all engagement takes place at the Board table in accordance with the agenda. A Board president with the help of the superintendent should make sure that civility and courtesy are extended to all in the Board room.

The most important role a superintendent and Board can play in their shared governance roles is to be transparent and honest with all internal and external stakeholders and the citizenry at large. Once trust is lost, it may be difficult to ever recover it again. The public is more forgiving of a Board and superintendent who acknowledge mistakes. The citizenry becomes distrusting when they learn of hidden issues and scandals "swept under the rug."

Building a Board Agenda

A School Board agenda should be carefully thought out and timelined. Meetings lasting more than two and a half hours can result in exhausting the Board's energy, resulting in restlessness. This is why it is important for the Board president to work with the superintendent in building the agenda. Here is a list of standing agenda items that will be reported on at most monthly Board meetings.

Board Agenda

- Call to Order
- Approval of Minutes
- Honors and Recognitions
- Student Board Member Reports (Nonvoting)
- Public Comment
- Instruction Report
- Building and Grounds Committee
- Finance Committe
- Policy Committee
- Communication Committee
- Treasurer Report
- Future Items for Next Meeting
- Adjournment
- Closed Session (only for restricted reasons allowable by state statutes)

Many school districts miss an opportunity to celebrate their successes. This is why honors and recognitions are so important to have on an agenda every month. It is an opportunity to bring honorees before the Board for certificates of recognition. There are always teacher and staff honors, student achievements, athletic honors, spelling bee and science fair champions, national merit scholars, or a community partnership recipient.

Filling the Board room at the beginning of the meeting to honor deserving recipients sets a positive tone. It also allows the press to do great picture stories with Board members congratulating honorees. As one superintendent commented, "No matter how tough a Board Meeting was going to be, I knew there would be something to cheer about during honors and recognitions!"

HELPING THE PRESS DO THEIR JOB

In many communities and school districts, the press (newspaper and local radio and cable television) may cover Board meetings. It is important for the Board and superintendent to make sure that accommodations for the press are in place. A Board and superintendent have to understand early on that the press has a job to do and deadlines to meet. While we may not always like the coverage or the slant that comes out at a Board meeting or from a controversial issue, the press deserves the cooperation of the Board and superintendent in reporting *all* the news. Nothing is more important to share with the citizens than the transparent truth, no matter how difficult it may be.

Many Board presentations are PowerPoints or media videos. For a reporter covering a Board meeting, it is helpful for a superintendent and other presenters to share a concise and brief executive summary with the reporter on each topic. In many cases, the reporter who is under deadline will copy and paste the executive summary account right into the article. This helps the reporter meet both the online and hard copy deadlines.

When planning any kind of celebration or newsworthy event, always invite the press and give them notice as far in advance as possible. In this day and age in which many people read online editions, we can't forget all of the senior citizens and others who still like a newspaper in their hands. There are also many people who like to listen to their hometown radio station for local news. Press releases and copy sent in advance to local media help the district in getting their great stories out to citizens. This is all a part of the communication agenda and keeping the public informed.

It is tough to take a beating in the press. Even some of the best superintendents and Boards have experienced some tough times when things have not played well in the press. This is only exacerbated when the Board or superintendent become adversarial and noncooperative with the press. The press will easily pick up on nontransparency or the appearance of hiding something. In short, it is far better to be forthright. Holding a grudge with the press never ends well. Take your lumps and move on! As one superintendent who had a long tenure pointed out, "The press purchases ink by the barrel. Far better to work with them. Pretty soon you will find they are much more an ally than an adversary."

POLICY: THE MOST IMPORTANT BOARD COMMITTEE

As mentioned at the very beginning of this chapter, in the shared governance roles of the Board and the superintendent, it is the Board that establishes and approves policy. Sound policy is needed for a school district to run smoothly.

With technology advances, emergency situations, instructional innovations, and new laws and state- and federal-level changes in education, policy is often being created or revised. In the past ten years, Boards have consistently had to revisit their appropriate use of technology policies. Issues like cyberbullying, sexting, and other misuses of social media often become national news. Sexual harassment and emergency plans with so many recent school shootings are constantly being revisited. Transgender policies have been reviewed and passed by many districts, but not without acrimony and controversy.

When a crisis or issue occurs, you want to be ready! If a policy is in place, then the superintendent and his or her team can carry out the appropriate administrative rules supporting the policy.

A district policy committee should meet regularly. At the beginning of the year it is advisable for a policy committee to create a list of policies that should be reviewed, along with new policies addressing anticipated issues. State Board of Education Associations often provide sample policies to help guide local Boards in their policy development.

A policy committee should be composed of at least two Board members and the superintendent. In addition, the superintendent should make sure that administrators and principals also serve on the committee depending on the nature of the policy (for example, instructional, financial, or safety). Often the director of instruction and the director of finance serve on the committee as the lead officers in working with the policy committee.

Any policy that is presented to the Board should be laid over for a month prior to final approval. This allows the public time to digest what has been presented and an opportunity to give feedback before the Board gives final approval. Some policies may take a couple of readings. Board members who are members of the policy committee should present the new or revised policy at the first reading. The superintendent and the administrative team can provide support or additional information, but it is the Board's role to present the new or revised policy.

Something to keep in mind is that school handbooks are an extension of Board policy. This can be easily overlooked. It is a good practice to have the Board approve all school handbooks, athletic codes, and activities handbooks prior to the beginning of a school year. Principals should present changes made annually in writing to the superintendent so he or she can then review and confirm the recommended changes are in compliance with current Board policy. In the case of suspension or expulsion appeals, a lawyer representing the student and parents will first examine if the punishment stated in the Board policy manual is consistent with the student handbook. It is embarrassing if there is a discrepancy.

MUTUAL TRUST: THE KEY TO GOOD BOARD
AND SUPERINTENDENT RELATIONSHIPS

In this chapter there was an attempt to present the roles and relationship between the Board and the superintendent. It comes down to trust and honest communication. A good superintendent treats all Board members equally and with respect. In a flourishing district, the Board stays out of micromanaging the day-to-day operations and focuses on policy, oversight, and student achievement. This as noted in this chapter as the *what*.

The superintendent and his or her educational team carry out the *how*. Once a Strategic Plan is approved and desired outcomes are established, it is the role of the superintendent and his or her team to carry out the goals and action plans.

There is a great sense of accomplishment and satisfaction on the part of Board members and superintendents when they come to the end of their terms or their tenure knowing they worked well together, respecting each other's role in shared governance.

SUMMARY QUESTIONS TO PONDER

- Are the roles and the relationships between the superintendent and the Board of Education clearly delineated in your school district?
- Is time and training invested into inducting new Board members in your school district?
- Do Board members in your district attend State Board of Education trainings and presentations to keep abreast of educational trends, court decisions, and policy advisement?
- Are Board members prepared and briefed on agenda items prior to a Board meeting?
- In the role of shared governance with the superintendent and administrative team, does your Board understand its role as holding the superintendent and administrators accountable for student achievement and continuous improvement?
- Does your Board keep its focus on policy rather than the day-to-day operations of the district and resist micromanagement?
- Is your Board of Education willing to approve task forces and ad-hoc committees to study and offer recommendations on issues of great local public interest?

Chapter Twelve

Life Balance

School leadership is demanding. There are some days and weeks when a principal, administrator, or superintendent may need to put in many more hours than usual. Time management is a challenge. As good as any leader might be, there comes a point when he or she must step back and assess if there is a serious imbalance among work, family, and personal time. Keeping a torrid work schedule pace is not healthy and can lead to burnout. Not only can our health suffer, but so too can relationships and families. We need to make sure that we take time away from work to decompress and enjoy the other facets of our lives that define us. Especially with our families and friends.

Some of our best thinking comes while we are exercising. Or some people now enjoy taking time to meditate. The key is not feeling selfish in taking some time for your own physical and mental well-being! A lot of nervous tension is released when we go for a swim, a run, a power walk, or to the gym. Yet this is the part of the day many principals and superintendents do not guard as sacred.

Hard pressed just to get one more thing off our list of tasks, we will forgo the time we set aside for ourselves. After a while this catches up with us. Before we know it, we become workaholics! Pretty soon the mindless eating and the pounds can add up. Marriages become strained, and our job performance dips. Leaders need time to refresh themselves; they are not machines that can go nonstop.

Unintentionally spending less time with our spouses, significant others, and family is an easy thing to do. You begin bringing home work for Saturdays and Sundays. Or you decide to stop by the office for an hour that turns out to be two or three hours. You are constantly looking at your texts and emails, and before you know it, you are spending an hour or more replying during what was intended to be personal time. We have to stay away from these traps!

One principal got to the point where he decided to date his wife. *"It was the one intentional way I could stop myself from taking time away from her. I literally carved out hours of time during the weekend and some weeknights where I wrote in 'date with wife.' I would like to say it always worked but it didn't. However, it made me a lot more conscious about not breaking the date."*

Time-consuming jobs in our society often place a strain on a marriage or a relationship. School leadership is not immune to this. Sadly, there are many principals and superintendents who have experienced divorces.

Here is another dirty dilemma the educational leadership professor mentioned in chapter 9, also shared with his students relating to life balance.

PREFACE: DIRTY DILEMMA POOR PATTY

Patty is the oldest of the O'Malley kids and pretty much set the bar for her four younger brothers and sisters. Mick O'Malley, her father, always bragged, "I never had to tell Patty to do something twice."

Patty at age twenty-four, two years out of college, married a fellow named Rick who she met at the University of Illinois in 1994. Both got jobs right out of college and began working in the Chicago Loop. The first two years of their marriage were bliss; they rode the train together downtown every morning, and they enjoyed all the fun things the city had to offer: sports, theater, great ethnic restaurants, museums, movies, and hanging out and having fun with their friends. Life was good.

They worked hard during the week and enjoyed their weekends and evenings together. In 1996 their first son, Tommy, was born. Patty stayed home for a few weeks then found a good babysitter, willing to come into the home. Their second child was born two years later in 1998. Patty still worked for the same advertising firm, and while the work was not challenging, they were good about giving her leave when Tommy was born, and now they were treating her very well in allowing her leave with little Megan.

Then things changed. Rick was a salesman for a software company. His job was now requiring more extensive travel. He was gone a lot. The fun weekends they were having when they were childless now seemed very busy. All of a sudden it seemed they needed more money and both needed to begin thinking about advancing their careers.

Over the next two years Rick really seemed to change. Fatherhood and being tied down did not seem to agree with him. More and more it seemed Patty and Rick were having arguments and disagreements. Pretty soon they were having dinners in silence. After an attempt to salvage the marriage with counseling, they divorced before their seventh wedding anniversary.

Patty, now almost thirty-two, decided to go back to school at night. After two tough years of working days, getting home to be with her kids, and having her mother babysit two nights a week, Patty earned her master's degree in business and marketing from DePaul University.

McGinty and Sons advertising firm, one of the most respected in the city, invites Patty in and hires her after her impressive interview. Within six months Patty earns a promotion. For the next several months her creative skills are being noticed by the top executives. Life is good again for Patty, she has bounced back. She has a live-in nanny who cares for Tommy and Megan when she is not home. Her mother also continues to be a great help to her. To top things off, she met a really nice guy by the name of Rudy during her train rides into the city. They first began by just talking to each other, and now they are dating. This guy seems so right. Patty's family and friends really like him as well.

Rudy asks Patty a couple of weeks before Labor Day weekend if she would like to go up to Door County for the long weekend. Gosh, does she want to go! She really likes Rudy, and for the past two years she has not spent a weekend away from home. He has really been understanding when she could not be away from her children. Subconsciously, she is afraid she could lose him. Mom seems to have this sized up. She says, "Go—I will take care of the kids, you have a great time!" Patty gives her mother a hug, calls Rudy, and tells him she is free to go thanks to Mom!

McGinty and Sons have been courting a million-dollar client, hoping to land their business. Helen the executive vice president comes into Patty's office on Wednesday and informs her that on the Saturday of Labor Day weekend, this client is coming in to see Mr. McGinty. Mr. McGinty insisted that Helen put together a team of three of their top writers and, to use his words exactly, "make sure you include that O'Malley girl!"

Patty does not know whether to laugh or cry. How should she handle this?

The professor opens the discussion: *Should Patty tell Rudy she can't go to Door County? Or should she tell Helen that she has a personal commitment over the Labor Day weekend that cannot be changed?*

In evaluating this case study, you probably came to a similar conclusion that most but not all of the professor's students arrived at. The students believed that Patty should tell Rudy of the client coming in and her boss's insistence on her being a part of the writing team. She should urge Rudy to hold off one day or reschedule the trip to Door County. If Rudy is truly a good guy he will understand and agree to alternative plans. After all, this is a big client! The boss himself wants Patty to be involved. She should not miss this opportunity to once again demonstrate her skill. It may indeed lead to further advancement of her career in this firm.

This case also touches on a gender issue. Are women asked to sacrifice their careers for the sake of the family or a relationship more often than men?

What is unique about this case is that Patty had a guardian angel who seemingly came out of nowhere. Helen the executive vice president had gotten to know Patty quite well and knew of her past struggles. She also knew how much she was looking forward to the Door County weekend. She convinced McGinty to reschedule the client to the following weekend. So Patty and Rudy enjoyed their long weekend in Door County!

While this seems like a simple case, the question becomes, "How many times do we give up a Saturday, a weekend, or our dinners and evenings during the week?" Time management can be a slippery slope for leaders. It is very easy to fall into the workaholic syndrome if one is not careful. Here are some tips to avoid this trap.

1. Use your vacation time. Some leaders never use up all of their vacation days. They sometimes carry them over or have the option of cashing them in. The saying "penny wise and pound foolish" comes into play here. You need to decompress and get refreshed. You will be sharper when you come back.
2. Not only use your vacation time but also try to get away. A trip, a cruise, or anywhere that people will not be inclined to disturb you.
3. Minimally try to make sure you have at least one of the weekend days totally free, not responding to email, texts, and phone calls (barring emergencies). This sounds hard but it works if one sticks to it.
4. During the week, make every effort to get home for dinner with your family. There may be some nights you can't, but try to keep these to a minimum.
5. If you do have to give up a weekend, make it up to your spouse, significant other, or family by maybe planning a weekend getaway.
6. Never miss a birthday or anniversary. If it falls on a school night when you have to work, then set up a day and date to really make the celebration special.

In summary, life balance is important. It takes discipline and planning to walk away from the job when that is exactly what you should do. Life is too short. We have to stop and smell the roses and have fun. Besides, work will always be there no matter how hard we try to stay ahead of things. In closing, we need to become experts in compartmentalizing work and our personal lives. We need to manage our time so we can find joy in all aspects of our life!

SUMMARY QUESTIONS TO PONDER

- Do you have hobbies, routines, or activities that allow you to decompress from your job at the end of the day?
- Has your job ever gotten in the way of important family or friendship priorities that you regret?
- Do you have the time management skills to control your calendar, allowing for family time?
- Do you exercise, eat right, and take care of yourself physically?
- Are you there for the important times and events of those you love?

Acknowledgments

I hope this book was helpful. As I mentioned in the introduction, this was not a scholarly work by any means. However, it was an effort on my part to share with you thirty-five years of K–12 leadership in public and private schools in urban, suburban, and rural communities.

My motivation for writing this book was to plant the seed that we need outstanding people leading our learning communities. If you are a good listener, sensitive, caring, and invested in your learning community, you can *lead and succeed!* Especially if you are committed to building a culture of leaders in which the capacity of teachers and staff is strengthened in a distributive leadership approach.

I could not have written this book had it not been for the love, guidance, and mentorship I have received throughout my life. It began with my father and mother, James and Annamae Fitzpatrick, who somehow raised eight kids. They provided love, guidance, and structure that enabled all of us to find our passions and pathways. The older I get, the more I ask myself, "How did they do it?" Well, I know the answer. They often denied themselves and sacrificed everything for us! I had to become a principal to really appreciate everything they did for us. In my career I have witnessed so many youths lacking the parental nurturing, guidance, and support that my siblings and I were so blessed to have.

I am also deeply indebted to the great teachers, mentors, coaches, university advisors, and bosses who taught and guided me through my journey.

I dearly love my children, Megan and Michael. I am proud of them for the people they are and the challenges they both have faced and overcome. Most of all I am proud that they are good people who throughout their lives have sought to help others.

My deepest gratitude is saved for my wife Therese Fitzpatrick. As of this writing, we have been married for forty-three years. She has stood by me through thick and thin. Throughout my career from teaching and coaching, to the principalship, to the superintendency, to collegiate professorial work, often necessitating moving and making a home in a new place. She has been my rock!

I love leadership, and we need passionate and strong leaders in our schools. You can be one of them. Hopefully this book served as a helpful guide and pathway to a leadership role you will cherish and find rewarding!

Bibliography

DuFour, R., and R. Marzano. 2011. *Leaders of Learning*. Bloomington, IN: Solution Tree Press.

Drucker, P. 2006. *The Effective Executive: The Definitive Guide to Getting the Right Things Done*. New York: HarperCollins Publishers.

Edwards, S., and P. Chapman. 2009. *Six Pillars of Dynamic Leadership*. Alexandria, VA: Educational Research Service.

Fullan, M. 2001. *Leading in a Culture of Change*. San Francisco: Jossey-Bass.

Fullan, M. 2014. *The Principal: Three Keys to Maximizing Impact*. San Francisco: Jossey-Bass.

Loftus, T. 1994. *The Art of Legislative Politics*. Washington, DC: CQ Press, a Division of Congressional Quarterly Inc.

Reeves, D. 2011. *Finding Your Leadership Focus*. New York: Teachers College Press.

Reeves, D. 2016. *From Leading to Succeeding: The Seven Elements of Effective Leadership in Education*. Bloomington, IN: Solution Tree Press.

About the Author

Dr. James Fitzpatrick (Jim) is an assistant professor at National Louis University (NLU) in Chicago, Illinois. He has been with NLU since 2014. In his role in the Educational Leadership Department he works with aspiring principals, superintendents, central office directors, and higher education candidates.

Jim attended St. Ambrose University in Davenport, Iowa, from 1971 to 1975, earning his bachelor of arts degree in history. Like in high school, he competed on the St. Ambrose cross-country and track teams. It was there that he met his future wife, Therese, who is also a graduate of St. Ambrose University and a professional educator of world languages.

Jim began his teaching career in the fall of 1975 at Newman Catholic High School in Mason City, Iowa. He was there from 1975 to 1980. During that time, he taught social studies and his cross-country teams were a state power, winning the state championship in the fall of 1979. He coached several Drake relay qualifiers and track champions during those years.

In 1980, Jim earned his master's degree in educational administration from the University of Iowa. He went on to serve in two Iowa principalships: in Lost Nation (as principal for grades 7 through 12) from 1980 to 1982 and at West Liberty High School from 1982 to 1986.

In the fall of 1986, Jim was appointed principal of Beloit Memorial High School in Beloit, Wisconsin, a position he would hold through 1997. Jim was an influential player in the passage of a $26.5-million-dollar referendum to renovate Beloit Memorial. He also played a key role in the planning and design of the four-hundred-and-sixty-thousand-square-foot facility. During his years in Beloit, Jim also became known as a national leader in the area of four-block scheduling and was a much sought after consultant in this area of school reform.

In May 1999, Jim earned his PhD in educational leadership and policy development. That same spring, Jim was appointed superintendent of the school district of Fort Atkinson, Wisconsin. He served that community for fourteen years until his retirement in June 2013. During his tenure, he led the district in the establishment and revising of Strategic Planning, the opening of Luther Elementary School, four-year-old kindergarten, and many other curriculum and fiscal initiatives. Under Jim's leadership the district passed several operational referendums during one of the most difficult political and economic periods Wisconsin has ever experienced. His leadership assured the district would be on sound fiscal footing in future years.

Through his frequent columns and newsletters Jim has been an activist in advocating for improved school funding and support of public education. He has also published articles in national and state educational journals related to school and district leadership.

Jim has been a sought after guest presenter and consultant in school districts and universities nationally. His presentation topics have included building strong administrative teams, promoting positive school culture, and four-block scheduling. He has also accepted several public speaking invitations as a motivational speaker for recognition programs and graduations.

Jim enjoys teaching at NLU. His goal is to build confidence in his students and provide mentorship. His quest is to give back to his students as his mentors did for him when he began his educational administration studies back in 1977.

Jim and his wife, Therese, live in Fort Atkinson, Wisconsin. They have two children, Megan who is married and lives and works in Chicago with her husband BJ, and Michael who, after serving in the United States Army, now lives and works in Madison, Wisconsin. Jim and Therese also have two grandsons, Jimmy and Paddy, who their dad (BJ Reid) is projecting as future draft choices of the Chicago White Sox!

Made in the USA
Monee, IL
07 October 2022